FIRE IN THE VEINS
NORFOLK REBELS

Joanna Lehmann-Hackett

FIRE IN THE VEINS
NORFOLK REBELS

Joanna Lehmann-Hackett

WP
WYMER
PUBLISHING
Bedford, England

First published in Great Britain in 2012
by Wymer Publishing
PO Box 155, Bedford, MK40 2YX
www.wymerpublishing.co.uk
Tel: 01234 326691

ISBN 978-1-908724-02-1

Edited by Jeremy Francis-Broom.

Every effort has been made to trace the copyright holders of the
photographs in this book but some were unreachable. We would
be grateful if the photographers concerned would contact us.

Original typesetting, layout and design by Amanda Lehmann.
Printed and bound by Lightning Source.

A catalogue record for this book is available from the British Library.

Cover design by Amanda Lehmann.
Photographs © Amanda Lehmann.
Illustrations © Amanda Lehmann & Joanna Lehmann-Hackett.

CONTENTS

Foreword

by Keith Skipper

I don't drive a car. I won't carry a mobile phone. I still use pen and ink and joined-up writing to contact family and friends. I vehemently oppose all changes blatantly imposed on Norfolk in an attempt to make it a boring photostat of everywhere else.

Yes, some of my virtues may be carved out of laziness and incompetence - and I don't mind progress as long as it doesn't alter anything - but there's no need to apologise for a rebellious streak in a blessed county where it has blossomed so prodigiously.

Of course, even the Queen of the Iceni, inventor of the wheelie-bin with knives, had to put up with the occasional cry of "cantankerous mawther!" while Tom Paine, early example of Thetford overspill, probably attracted the odd "What are yew loike!" on his international travels.

I recall being kicked off the Norwich City team bus by an irate Carrow Road manager who wanted me to be more of a subservient supporter and less of an independent-minded reporter.

I parted regular company with the BBC - it was their idea - after refusing to apologise for an article I'd written about the loss of local flavour in local radio output.

It can be tough taking on the role of prophet without honour on your own midden, but there's no point in boasting principles if they bend or break on the merest breeze of expediency.

This compelling volume brings together a host of colourful characters determined to take the Norfolk mantra of "dew diffrunt" to new levels... and so make a difference on or beyond native soil. We must admire and celebrate them all for defying the odds.

I cherish meetings and mardles with some of my inspirations along the busy Norfolk way.

Dialect enthusiasts like schoolmaster and naturalist Dick Bagnall-Oakeley, who taught at Gresham's in Holt, one of the area's poshest schools, but had the courage and flair to give our precious local vernacular a prominent platform in high places.

I salute Dick Condon, the genial Irishman who turned Norwich Theatre Royal into one of the most successful theatres in Europe while showing how blarney and cordiality could live alongside business and culture.

Allan Smethurst, the Singing Postman, took Norfolk into the national pop charts with his romantic take on girls who smoke too much. He had no rivals in Tin Pan Alley when it came to warbling about cockles, samphire, steam trains, a nice loaf of bread and horn-rimmed glasses. There's a showbiz rebel for you!

Ted Ellis, the people's naturalist, was an expert without airs, a celebrity who remained a modest man despite remarkable achievements. And my farm labourer father told me all about George Edwards, that inspiring son of the soil who did so much to improve conditions for those who worked on Norfolk's fertile acres.

Just a few of the more recent additions to the great panoply of outstanding figures who did it their way, often with a smile that hinted: "You can always tell a Norfolk man or woman, (adopted or home-grown) - but you can't tell 'em much!"

Keith Skipper
Cromer, 2011

Introduction

A Romantic Rebel's Perspective Of Norfolk

by Steve Hackett

From the sense of freedom I felt as child and a Londoner visiting Yarmouth for the first time, running on the pier against the bracing wind in the face of the turbulent North Sea waves, I have always loved Norfolk. It appears tranquil in its beautiful rolling countryside, but there is another side to this place...

Norfolk has never ceased to amaze me. One of my most extraordinary experiences of the place was in the small village of West Runton on the North Norfolk coast. It's amazing to think that its venue West Runton Pavillion could once have been a magnet for some of the most unruly pop and rock 'n' roll groups, from Thin Lizzy, Motorhead and Iron Maiden through to the Sex Pistols! In 1983 my own rock band was welcomed into this inner sanctum of rebellion. I have to say that it was one of my most enjoyable gigs. It may have been small, but the audience went wild in the spirit of every true Norfolk Rebel, and the atmosphere was literally electric. I was sad to hear about the venue's closure in 1986 and I recently attended a reunion.

I continue to play in Norfolk, most recently to a fun crowd at a melting pot of many rebellious ideas and activities, the University of East Anglia, and my wife Jo Lehmann and I spend a lot of time with her family in the area.

Jo and I love to stand on the cliff tops on a stormy day and watch the spray smashing over the rocks below. You only have to glimpse the ever changing skies on the open coast to get a sense of the wildness that underpins the land. It's not hard to imagine how pirates and smugglers once ruled those rugged shores, and this book brings to life the ever changing face of this landscape of rebellion over the last 2000 years.

Digging into the history of Norfolk with its heroes, heretics, martyrs and mavericks, I can see how the county of Norfolk has shaped world events from Thomas Paine to Nelson and to many who lost their lives in the cause of their beliefs with fire indeed burning inside their veins. Jo's heartfelt book brings those people back to life and invites you to an Odyssey through time, following the insistent spirit of rebellion that has ignited hearts and minds globally throughout the centuries.

Steve Hackett

Preface

Rebellion is the cause of chaos, pain and, sometimes, death. It is also the instigator of change. Those who conquer their fears and stand up against established ways and widely held views invariably sacrifice a quiet life for a dangerous fight for what they believe in. The actions of rebels make the world today a dramatically different place from what it might otherwise have been. For better or for worse, life rarely stands still in the face of rebellion.

Today, influenced by the media, we tend to think of rebels in far off places like Iraq, Uzbekistan or the Sudan. Over the centuries many rebels have also risen up in Britain, with violence equal to any we see in other countries today. Thousands have died in the fight for their causes.

The quiet face of Norfolk gives the appearance of a backwater that has changed little for centuries. But this most easterly of England's counties has a history of dissent and upheaval.

A Norfolk woman once challenged the strength of the Roman Empire, and a Norfolk man helped to inspire and instigate the American Revolution.
Norfolk's rebels have transformed life in the county, and in many cases have had a powerful influence on national and international events.

Norfolk has been a surprising hotbed of subversion and rebellion. This book tells the stories of Norfolk's rebels, many of them linked, and weaves them into the vibrant tapestry of rebellion that is our inheritance.

Chapter One

WHEN BLOOD SOAKED THE LAND

When Blood Soaked The Land

VIOLENCE FOR JUSTICE

Norfolk appears to be a particularly tame part of Britain, with its picturesque villages, woods, Broads and flat or gently rolling fields. Yet, beneath the tranquillity lies a turbulent past. Who could guess that in a battle in the town of North Walsham, many were massacred, or that thousands of rebels once took over Norwich? It is even harder to imagine that it was the people of Norfolk who laid waste to London, and fought the Roman army in one of the most impressive battles of history.

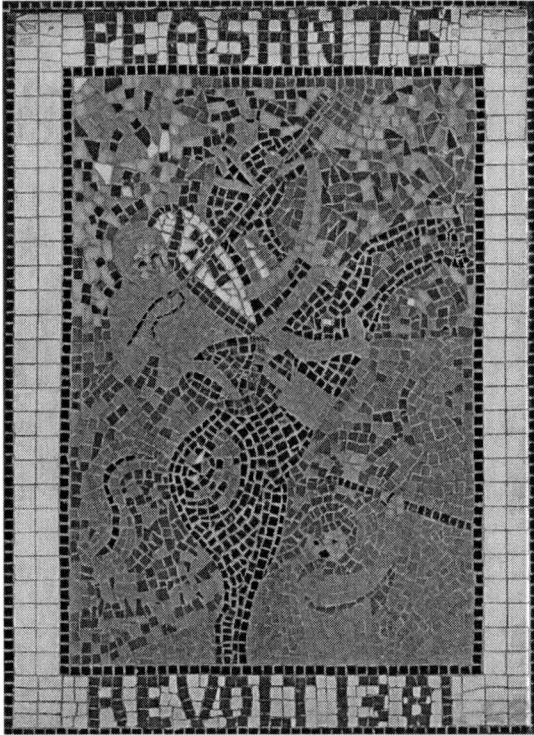

Peasants revolt, North Walsham

The woman who took on an empire

Two thousand years ago the Iceni, who inhabited the region covering the whole of Norfolk and over the border into what is now Suffolk, took pride in their sense of identity and independence, as Norfolk people still do today. These were times when violence was the only way to gain control or autonomy, and so it seemed to the Iceni who took on the mighty Roman power that ruled Britain.

Boudica, the tall redheaded Iceni queen who led the uprising in AD 60, was a rebel with a cause. The Iceni had earlier risen in revolt when the Romans confiscated weapons from all southern British men. This time the stakes were much higher.

Boudica's husband Prasutagus had left half his kingdom to the Romans and the rest to his queen and their two daughters. The Romans refused to recognise Iceni female rights to rule, and determined to take control over the Iceni kingdom. Roman soldiers pillaged Iceni homes, flogged Boudica and raped her daughters. Estates were removed from Iceni chieftains and Prasutagus's family members were enslaved.

Enraged at the violation against herself, her family and her realm, the feisty Boudica roused the Iceni to revolt. With the support of the Trinovantes to the south, they burned Colchester, the Roman-British capital, to the ground, and sacked both London and St. Albans. The rebel fighters were a wild bunch whose rage knew no bounds.

The Roman historian Tacitus claimed that 70,000 Roman citizens died at the hands of this barbarian horde. According to reports, around 250,000 rebels confronted only 400 Roman soldiers in battle some miles north of St Albans along Watling Street. Nevertheless, the Romans – well organised and skilled in military tactics - won an overwhelming victory. Boudica disappeared from records and it is believed that she may have poisoned herself. The Romans burned and ravaged the whole Norfolk area, and survivors faced starvation.

The Iceni, whose kingdom was centred around Thetford, did not dare to rebel against the Romans again. But their spirit of proud independence was to re-emerge years later.

Boudica statue in Westminster

Norwich Castle under siege

Turbulent times followed the Roman departure of around AD 410, with invasions by Saxons, Vikings, Danes and Angles (the latter giving their name to East Anglia as well as to England). Despite the influx of foreigners, a strong sense of local identity remained and re-emerged soon after the Norman Conquest of 1066. In 1075 Ralph, Earl of Norfolk and Suffolk, son of a Breton mother and a Norfolk father, joined Roger de Breteuil, Earl of Hereford in a revolt to overthrow William the Conqueror, whose sheriffs were undermining their traditional rights. Ralph went to Denmark to seek help, leaving his wife Emma to defend Norwich Castle. William's troops burned the houses of Ralph's supporters in and around Norwich and besieged the castle.

Emma held out for three months. Under the pressure of the onslaught and her own increasingly disaffected and rowdy bunch of men, she seized the opportunity of promised safe conduct and made her get-away to Brittany. Having failed to rally the Danes in time, Ralph joined her and continued the fight against William the Conqueror from there.

The people rise up

Like Boudica, the Earl of Norfolk and his wife Emma were people of high status who felt compelled to fight in order to maintain local independence and control. However, as the Norman and Saxon cultures in Britain merged over the three or four hundred years following the Norman conquest, many of the major violent rebellions were instigated by oppressed 'underdogs' against the increasingly rich élite, rather than by powerful and wealthy individuals. Chapter 4 describes how Norfolk people rose up more and more against the power and wealth of the monasteries and of the Catholic Church in general. Along with the suffering caused by the Black Death, war and famine, the resentment of ordinary people against the élite and the Church was a major factor underlying the 1381

Norwich Castle still dominates the city today

Peasants' Revolt. The last straw to spark the revolt was the crippling poll tax.

A large crowd from Kent and Essex led by Wat Tyler stormed London to seek concessions from Richard III. Norfolk was one of the few areas to stage its own local rebellion, led by a dyer from Framlingham, John (or Geoffrey) Litester. His band of rebels sent emissaries to London, but the 'Warrior' Bishop Despenser of Norwich intercepted them. The Bishop was a bloodthirsty character bent on eliminating any remotely rebellious faction or individual.

Litester and his men gathered on Mousehold Heath, where they set up camp overlooking Norwich. They killed two aristocrats, went on the rampage looting wealthy houses in Norwich and Great Yarmouth, and burned various manor court rolls recording feudal obligations.

One particular target was John Reed, the collector of poll tax at Rougham. The rebels broke into his house and looted it. They also excitably pursued clergyman Edmund Gurnay to the coast because he was the steward of the detested and enormously rich and powerful John of Gaunt, Duke of Lancaster (1340-1399). Gurnay and John Holkham, a justice, seized a boat to make their escape. The rebels found another boat and continued the chase until night fell and Gurnay and Holkham escaped and secretly landed at Burnham under cover of darkness.

Litester and his men took great pleasure in turning the tables on their wealthy people that they took captive, making them serve and grovel at their feet. Their lack of respect for established authority was a general feature of the Peasants' Revolt. Some of the participants broke into the Tower of London, found their way to the Queen's bedroom and proceeded to jump up and down on her bed!

North Walsham church massacre

Although the demoralising news of the Peasants' Revolt leader, Wat Tyler's death in London, and the failure of the main revolt undermined the Norfolk campaign early on, Litester held out on Mousehold Heath for almost two weeks. By then Bishop Despenser had rallied his troops and the holy sword-wielder finally crushed the rebellion in the battle of North Walsham. Thousands were slain as the rebels fled, and

North Walsham Church where rebels were massacred

a few hundred ran into the town church for sanctuary. However, knowing that the church was newly built and not yet consecrated, Despenser and his men had no qualms about bursting in and massacring the rebels. Litester was captured and subsequently hung, drawn and quartered. Despenser personally presided over the procedure and saw to it that parts of Litester's body were put on display at North Walsham, King's Lynn, Great Yarmouth and Norwich as a warning to anyone considering rebellion.

Despite the way in which the Peasants' Revolt was so thoroughly crushed, the urge to fight the in the face of starvation, end serfdom, gain more freedom and reduce tax was not diminished. Following bad harvests, there were two riots in Norfolk in the 1520s. And when there was unrest in other parts of England, Norfolk was invariably ready to play its part.

Norfolk's doomed hero

In 1549 groups formed around England to take a stand against land enclosures by wealthy landowners who, in extending their holdings, were squeezing out the poorer ones. Some of these groups rioted, but generally accepted a pardon from the authorities in exchange for a promise of concessions. But not in Norfolk! There the rebels refused the pardon, further escalating the revolt.

Robert Kett, a landowner and tanner from Wymondham, led a group of rebels to Norwich where he too camped on Mousehold Heath. Like Litester and his men, Kett took pleasure in turning the tables. Immortalised in a mural at the Castle Mall in Norwich, a young boy in Kett's camp could not resist presenting his naked behind to a visiting royal herald! Again like Litester, Kett gained the support of some Norwich folk, described as 'a great rowt of the lewd citizens', to swell the rebel numbers. The force of numbers helped Kett to defeat the Marquis of Northumberland in battle, and for a month Kett held sway over Norwich. Kett's supporters were made up mainly of the urban poor who resented not only the high taxes they were forced to pay, but also their rich overlords who often squeezed the homes of the poor into ever tighter spaces as they extended their large city houses. In the country, rural landowners were taking over large tracts of land, mainly for sheep farming. Though Kett was himself a wealthy landowner, he

Colegate - the scene of a "great riot" during Kett's Rebellion

had a social conscience and threw his support behind the small farmers who were losing their land and jobs. Protector Somerset, who made decisions on behalf of the young King Edward, had moved to limit land enclosures, and Kett was insisting on the enforcement of that policy.

Having camped on Mousehold Heath for seven weeks, Kett and his rebel group, estimated to be 20,000 strong, were defeated after three days of heavy fighting pitched against the Earl of Warwick and his army. Kett escaped, only to be caught a few hours later. His brother William was hanged at Wymondham church, while Robert Kett was left dangling from a gibbet at Norwich Castle until his body rotted, as a warning to potential rebels. For years afterwards, the end of Kett's uprising on 27th August was a day on which Norwich citizens were expected to reflect on the evils of rebellion. However, over the last couple of centuries as social change gathered pace, Kett has been increasingly recognised as a hero and an inspiration. A plaque at Norwich Castle commemorates him.

Kett's Oak where Kett alledgedly spoke to his followers

A Norwich tavern reminds of Kett's passage from rebel to hero

In spite of constant reminders of the horror of Kett's defeat, within a hundred years Norfolk people were again in rebellious mood. The principal battles of the Civil War were not on Norfolk turf, but Norfolk people left the county to join the fighting. Moreover, there were revolts, numerous plots and sixteen executions in Norwich alone for mutiny and rebellion, along with a number of major riots.

Following the sacking of the cathedral, celebrated with enthusiasm by Norwich citizens in

1643, there was a change of emphasis. Ravaged by plague, religious division and under the burden of heavy taxation to pay for war, people began to riot against their parliamentarian overlords. The riots culminated in the 'Big Blow', a massive gunpowder explosion that, with the cathedral sacking, is described in Chapter 4.

Rebellion of the 'nobs'!

Unrest was widespread but King's Lynn was the only Norfolk town to rebel in a major way against the parliamentarian Eastern Alliance. In 1643, encouraged by the successes of Newcastle's royalist forces, King's Lynn openly declared its support for Charles I. One of the royalist gentry, Sir Hamon L'Estrange, (1583-1654), was appointed governor. The town came under siege as parliamentarian forces fought to regain control. Lives were lost and fighting continued until, under the threat of a crippling bombardment, the royalist leaders capitulated. The unruly Lynn soldiers were reluctant to lay down their arms and were not readily pacified.

The surrender of King's Lynn quietened royalist rebellions but the cost of war, reflected again in high taxes, rekindled support for the loyalist cause over the next few years. In 1650 a group of Norfolk royalists plotted to take Norwich, while others had similar ideas for Downham Market, Swaffham and Thetford. Constrained by insufficient men to carry the plans through, the leaders were caught and executed. Thomas Cooper, an ex-clergyman schoolmaster from Holt who was among those condemned, was executed outside the school door on Christmas Day. The puritan parliamentarians were a 'baa, humbug!' bunch who saw Christmas celebrations as debauched, so they clearly chose that day especially for the hanging. This incident highlights the inequitable treatment of rich and poor, with an ordinary person like Thomas Cooper being executed while Sir Hamon L'Estrange, who had led the bloody King's Lynn rebellion, merely had his estates sequestered. A poor man could be hanged for stealing a pair of shoes!

Tuesday Market, King's Lynn
A monument to a thriving port and commercial centre

Again the tables turn

Before the Civil War, the upright King's man Sir Hamon would never have envisaged himself a rebel. But in times of war and rebellion, the definition of a rebel can become blurred. Miles Corbet of Sprowston, a loyal supporter of Cromwell's government, was subsequently captured and hanged once Charles II was on the throne. Corbet had been the only Norfolk man to sign Charles I's death warrant, and so is referred to as Norfolk's regicide. After the Restoration of 1660, he was viewed as a dangerous rebel and his remains were displayed on London Bridge, the customary warning to any aspiring social deviant. In Corbet's view, the restoration of the monarchy had brought on a 'deluge of profanes of whoredoms swearing cursings drunkenness poperie prelacie malice raige and bitterness'!

Discontent was never far beneath the surface, and the suffering at its root continued. Many thousands died from the outbreak of plague during the first ten years of Charles II's reign, and over the next 100 years bad harvests, followed by increasing unemployment and poverty led to a number of riots, particularly in Norwich. The situation worsened with the cost of the American War of Independence, followed by war with France between 1793 and 1815.

Many Norwich citizens were not prepared to put up with the prohibitive taxes, and following their rebellious tradition, some sympathised with the French revolutionaries. Radical clubs sprang up, pushing for peace or rousing people to 'join and rebel' and to 'Meet with Hundreds to begin a Glorious Revolution'. The Norwich Revolution Society, formed to support the French Revolution, became increasingly opposed to the wealthy élite. Once England had declared war on France, action was taken against the society and its secretary Isaac Saint was arrested. Norwich was branded as 'that city of sedition'. Antagonism between Whigs (who later becme the Liberals) and Tories was particularly strong in the city, and general elections periodically led to rioting and punch-ups.

Starvation, arson and mayhem

As war with France groaned on, increasing poverty exacerbated discontent and by the time it finally ended, many soldiers had problems finding employment and wages were lowered. About ten thousand rioters in Norwich pelted Member of Parliament Thomas William Coke with stones, in opposition to the new Corn Law. Agricultural riots broke out in various parts of Norfolk. George Fortis, arrested in 1822, was accused of setting fire to haystacks. He protested that he had fought as a loyal citizen and soldier for seven years, and his only offence was to steal some firewood. Nevertheless, he was hanged in front of a large excitable crowd outside Norwich Castle.

Despite harsh punishment for rebellious actions, desperation drove people to continued rioting. Over 3,000 Norwich weavers hurled looms from the workhouse into the river, the Catton saw mills were destroyed, and across the county mobs attacked and disabled machines and fired haystacks. Food riots broke out, with starving labourers attacking corn mills and farmers.

At this time, Norfolk was one of the most troubled areas of the country. The riots did not subside until after 1870 when the trade union movement began to grow, giving protesters an official and more effective voice. Riots became more isolated incidents, such as the suffragette cause (Chapter 2) or the fight for Argyle Street (Chapter 7), and few large violent rebellions took place in the late nineteenth and early twentieth centuries.

Desperation leading to rioting

Norfolk's history shows that violence erupted whenever there appeared to be no other option, or when desperation, anger and a gross sense of injustice reached boiling point.

The independence of Norfolk people coupled with their experience of great hardship, goes a long way to explaining why Norfolk can claim so many rebels. From Boudica, through to Litester, Kett and more recent figures, Norfolk rebels have put their lives on the line for the greater good, making their mark on history and moulding Norfolk as it is today.

Chapter Two

HYENAS IN PETTICOATS
AND ANGELS IN THE DOCK

Hyenas In Petticoats And Angels In The Dock

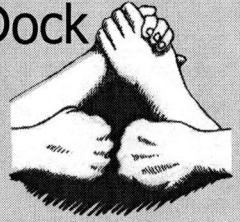

THE STRUGGLE FOR SOCIAL REFORM

The riots and rebellions in Norfolk continued well into the nineteenth century, instigated largely by downtrodden agricultural workers and wool weavers. But by the late eighteenth century a growing number of people had decided that non-violent ways could be a more effective path for reform. An influx into Norfolk of persecuted Low Country Calvinists and, later, French Huguenots served to strengthen an already thriving tradition of religious and social dissent in the area.

Norfolk also provided fertile ground for the development and settlement of nonconformist groups like the Unitarians and the Quakers, who had strong social and religious principles. The English Civil War had nurtured radical ideas such as social equality and women's rights, and many people were later inspired by the ideals of the French Revolution. By the early nineteenth century Norwich had become such a hotbed of subversive thinking that it was not only referred to as a 'city of sedition', but also as the Athens of England, based on the original thinking of a growing intelligentsia.

From 'Godless Billy' to a charge of high treason

Amongst the nonconformist Norwich radicals was the scholar William Taylor (1765-1836). He was critical of bible scriptures and vocal in his support for universal suffrage. He made his left-wing views widely known and supported the French Revolution even after England had turned against the new French Republic.

A religious, social and political rebel, Taylor earned the nickname of 'Godless

Norwich, the "Athens of England"

22

Billy'! He drank heavily with his friends, a factor which led the Norwich born writer Harriet Martineau to criticise his set as 'ignorant and conceited' men who believed they could solve the world's problems through their 'destructive propensities'. In spite of her assessment, Taylor was taken seriously by other political radicals such as William Wordsworth and Samuel Taylor Coleridge, who appreciated his literary translations.

The Tower of London: the end of the line for many rebels

The Norwich radicals invited well-known political activists from all over the country to address their meetings. One such activist, John Thelwall, visited Norwich to campaign for the vote. Soldiers invaded the meeting, and in Yarmouth a bunch of sailors attempted to attack him, wounding many bystanders. On both occasions he escaped. The authorities feared that he might influence the military to turn against the government, in support of a revolution. Coming soon after the French Revolution, their fears were strong and led to the repression of many radical thinkers. Thelwall was eventually imprisoned in the Tower of London on a charge of high treason, along with fellow reformers Thomas Hardy and John Horne Tooke.

The dissenting intelligentsia

Horne Tooke had the admiration of Norwich doctor John Alderson, a Unitarian referred to as the hub of the 'dissenting intelligentsia', and his daughter Amelia, later to become the writer Amelia Opie (1769-1853). Amelia Opie was often present during Horne Tooke's trial and is said to have given him a kiss to congratulate him on his acquittal!

Amelia and her father were close to some of the most revolutionary thinkers of the time. They criticised society and upheld the ideals of freedom and equality. One of these friends was William Godwin, whose philosophy was damned by many as radical heresy. Amelia grew close to Godwin's lover Mary Wollstonecraft, who had spent time in France during the revolution and was a strong advocate of women's rights. Amelia's interest in politically and socially rebellious ideas was evident in *Adeline Mowbray*, the book she later wrote based on Wollstonecraft's life. However, they knew each other for only a short time before Wollstonecraft's death soon after giving birth to her daughter, who was to become Mary Shelley, author of *Frankenstein*.

With her father derided and her mother demonised after her death as a serpent, prostitute or 'hyena in petticoats', it is hardly surprising that Shelley would be haunted by monstrous imagery. Amelia Opie was aware of the slanders and had observed more than one acquaintance being tried for treason. These experiences were perhaps behind her decision to withdraw her support from the most fiery of the revolutionary rebels after Wollstonecraft's death. She married the painter John Opie at this time, and his circle tended to be more moderate. Nonetheless, she still shared radical ideas with her friends in the Norwich based Quaker Gurney family, and like them she was a particularly strong supporter of the anti-slavery movement.

Amelia Opie: a life influenced by revolutionary thinkers

Squalor, slavery and death exposed

Sir Thomas Fowell Buxton (1786-1845), who married Hannah Gurney, lived for many years in the North Norfolk village of Northrepps, and was a major player in the movement. As a Member of Parliament, he opposed the tradition of slavery in the British colonies, and led the campaign after William Wilberforce's death. Buxton spoke out against the horrific conditions in the slave ships, where only one in three survived, describing them as 'horrible, stinking, floating hells'. He met with strong opposition, but eventually achieved success with the passage through Parliament in 1833 of the Slavery Abolition Act. Not satisfied with his achievements, he continued to push for better conditions in Africa and beyond.

Buxton also campaigned to abolish the deeply ingrained system of capital punishment. Despite heavy resistance, his efforts led to a massive reduction in the number of crimes that led to the death penalty. Buxton raised a large sum of money to support the struggling weavers who lived in appalling squalor in London. He also supported his wife's sister Elizabeth Fry in her fight to change prison conditions, as she supported him in his stand against capital punishment.

Slave ships - 'horrible, stinking, floating hells'

The Angel of Mercy

It is easy to think of people like Thomas Fowell Buxton and Elizabeth Fry as reformers rather than rebels. But they fought for changes to age-old ways of doing things; their ideas were truly revolutionary and they were often viewed as dangerously rebellious or subversive. When Elizabeth and her brother Joseph Gurney tried to save from the gallows a woman who had been pressured into passing forged bank notes, the Home Secretary Lord Sidmouth accused Fry and Gurney of threatening to remove 'the dread of punishment in the criminal classes'.

Elizabeth Fry (1780-1846) was born a Gurney in Norwich and brought up mainly at the family home of Earlham Hall, now part of the University of East Anglia (UEA). She was a nervous child, only beginning to display a rebellious streak in her late teens. She found the family's religious meetings boring and wore what were considered inappropriately bright clothes and footwear. Later, she was deeply impressed by William Savery, a visiting Quaker preacher from the United States, who was a strong proponent of social responsibility and who anticipated that she would follow an important calling.

Elizabeth, who became known as the Angel of Mercy, resolved to dedicate her life to the Quaker tradition of philanthropy. She actively helped a number of

Earlham Hall, the home of the Gurney family

impoverished communities and the inmates of 'lunatic asylums' and hospitals; but her principle work was in the prisons. Quakers had been persecuted and imprisoned in the seventeenth century for their nonconformity, a cause that would have been close to her heart. Visiting Newgate Prison, she saw people starving in cramped and dirty conditions, where women in rags carried naked babies.

She was deeply disturbed by the psychological agony of those awaiting the death sentence. As well as confronting Lord Sidmouth on the hanging issue, she drummed up support to provide education and clothing for female prisoners. For years she worked tirelessly to improve the conditions of those being transported to Australia. She gave education and a sense of purpose to the women on the boats, and helped to establish a refuge for prisoners arriving in Australia, where they were given a chance to find work and freedom. She corresponded with Caroline Chisholm, the assertive, socially conscious wife of an English army officer who moved from India to Sydney, about the need for convict women to be supported. Mrs Chisholm, in an effort to increase the new colony's female population campaigned in Britain and Ireland for 'free female emigration', and on the women's arrival found them shelter and employment.

Elizabeth Fry was not afraid to stand against the cruelty of the established system or to confront the most intimidating of authoritarian figures. The frightened little girl who had been plagued by nightmares of drowning and too nervous to paddle in the sea at Cromer had become one of the most courageous and influential women in history. Now a national figure, her image is on the £5 note.

The golden age of philanthropy

The Mustard Shop in Norwich: a Colman family reminder

The Gurneys actively supported schools and hospitals, as did other nonconformist families and groups, creating places of education and care for the disadvantaged. The Colman family - of mustard fame - was another such benefactor. Breaking with tradition, they developed an extensive welfare programme for the Colman family workers and their families, including schools, low cost meals, medical and social care, and cheap accommodation. Much of this work was due to the efforts of James Jeremiah Colman, a nonconformist liberal who ran the family business for many years.

With other like-minded people, including the political radical Jacob Henry Tillett, the Colmans were among the instigators of the *Norfolk News*, later to become the *Eastern Daily Press (EDP)*. Concerned about social liberty, they advocated the vote for every man, education for all and the repeal of the Corn Laws. The *Norfolk News* helped to spread word of the first union to push for the rights of agricultural workers, set up by Joseph Arch in 1872. In his drive to improve social conditions, J. J. Colman was supportive of the union, flying in the face of many of the land-owning farmers who supported the status quo.

The *Norfolk News'* second editor James Spilling had been a radical and an enthusiastic supporter of the Chartist movement in his youth. He had acquired a pike in readiness for a potential revolution! By the time he became editor he believed the power of the written word to be a more sensible way to help the oppressed. During his time, the newspaper often attacked bad living conditions in Norwich.

The notorious Aylsham workhouse

Crow-scarer turned champion of the oppressed

Joseph Arch's union had the active support of George Edwards, a man from the North Norfolk village of Marsham. Edwards eventually became an MP, but he began his working life, aged six, as a crow scarer. Even as a small child he was deeply concerned to help his family, who were so poor and malnourished that his father had been driven to steal turnips for their survival and had been forced into hard labour as a punishment. Branded as a thief, he was unable to find employment and the family was consigned for a time to the notorious Aylsham workhouse.

As an adult, George Edwards was appalled by the landowners' persecution of those who supported Arch's union, laying them off work and turning them out of their cottages. He too was given notice to leave his job and was evicted with his family. He later wrote that his 'whole soul revolted against such tyranny'. Anger and violence were rife on all sides. At one union meeting in Norfolk, a young farmer rode in and tried to strike Arch with a whip-stalk. He was promptly unhorsed by Arch's supporters and thrown into a pond!

A nineteenth century Norfolk folk song succinctly puts the sentiments of the unionists:

> They would drive over poor folks
> Who stand in the way
> You slave-driving farmers
> You pot-bellied farmers
> You're forced to give way
> To the labouring man.

The agricultural unions made some gains, but fell apart under the strain of the depression at the end of the century. Still determined to fight for people's rights, Edwards nominated himself to stand for the Norfolk County Council. But he faced antagonism from the ruling classes who felt threatened by the revolutionary idea of a working man in a position of power. He became the victim of abuse, bags of flour and soot! Later, he succeeded in being elected to a parish council, and pushed hard for improved wages, and better conditions for widows, the aged, large families, girls in confinement and tramps. In his own words, Edwards was 'a rebel, out for revolution, to upset law and order' - a sentiment shared by many of his contemporaries.

By the early 1900s Edwards decided it was time to create a solid union for the long term. He set about organising the Agricultural Workers Union. This was a great success, and spread from Norfolk to the rest of the country. Edwards went from strength to strength, finally becoming a Labour MP in 1920. He had managed in spite of repeated opposition and victimisation to break old patterns and to improve significantly the life of labourers and other oppressed groups.

The school of freedom

When George Edwards stood for county council elections in 1910, his old friend Tom Higdon helped him. It was Edwards who then supported Higdon and his wife Kitty when in 1914 they were sacked from the Burston School where they taught. This led to the longest strike in the country's history, the Burston School strike, which Edwards referred to as 'a great fight for religious and political freedom.'

A farmer-dominated committee dismissed the Higdons for helping the Agricultural Workers Union recruit new members, and for opposing farmers who removed children from school to help with the harvest. The two teachers believed strongly in independence of spirit, equality and justice, and were not afraid to fly in the face of authority to uphold their ideals. Their pupils went on strike in support of their sacked teachers, valuing their encouragement of individual expression. They continued their education on the village green under the tutelage of the Higdons. Parents were fined and many were evicted from their homes. Trade unionists and social reformers donated money, and the 'School of Freedom' was built. Today the old Burston School is a museum of the strike, and every year a rally is held to celebrate its establishment.

Strikes around the turn of the twentieth century were due mainly to low wages, and centred mostly on Norwich where the problem was most chronic as wages had been driven down by the influx of unemployed labourers into the city during the agricultural depression. This was one of the factors that accounted for the shift from liberalism to labour. Many nonconformists felt let down when Lloyd George's Liberal government did not satisfy their hopes for pacifism and equality in education and religion. Conditions for many were still very tough, and people welcomed the Labour Party's focus on social welfare.

A new realm of ideals

One woman to rebel against the liberal tradition of her family was Dorothy Jewson (1884-1964). Concerned about local social conditions and believing that

George Edwards & (inset) Burston School

radical change was necessary, she expressed her ideas in a book, *The Destitute of Norwich* and was Labour MP for Norwich in 1923-4. She advocated birth control, then a contentious issue, and pushed for women's voting age to be reduced to 21. In her early years she was a suffragette. Norfolk suffragettes are said to have smashed windows and burned buildings, including the Britannia Pier in Great Yarmouth, but no evidence has been found that Jewson was involved in any of these militant activities. She was a pacifist and opposed to Britain being a part of the First World War (Chapter 3).

Dorothy Jewson was involved with many of the ideas and movements that became important during the twentieth century. She often clashed with the establishment and sometimes had strong disagreements with members of her own party, including Joseph

Chamberlain who opposed her stand on birth control. She had influence; this was an era when a woman pushing for social ideals and women's rights would no longer be dismissed and demonised as a 'hyena in petticoats'.

Norwich-born Henry Massingham (1860-1924) also stood firm against war, in his case the Boer War and the First World War. He too switched his allegiance to the Labour Party, believing it to be a force for social change. He was a journalist with the *Eastern Daily Press* and later an editor. With contributions from radical thinkers such as George Bernard Shaw he later made a success of the national newspaper *The Star*.

Norwich has remained a hotbed of radical thinking into the 21st century. Ian Gibson, previously Dean of Biology at UEA and since 1992 Labour MP for Norwich North, does not follow the party line on a number of key issues. He fought strongly against the Government's policy on university top-up fees, over which he clashed with Norwich South MP Charles Clarke, then Secretary for Education. Gibson also opposed both the push for identity cards and for military action in Iraq.

The enormous leaps forward made in social terms between the eighteenth and twentieth centuries were hard fought for by principled rebels. In some cases, opposition became a spur for rebellion. Threatened by repression and persecution, men like George Edwards stood firm and fought even harder. Elizabeth Fry became ever more determined in the face of the resistance of prison governors and the Home Secretary's disapproval. They were all pushing against the ingrained habits of a 'crusty' system run by people reluctant to part with power or wealth, or to deal with the social ills of the day, regarding them as normal. Suffering and poverty and the upheavals of the Industrial Revolution aroused labourers to battle for justice and survival. They and intellectual radicals were influenced and encouraged by the American and French Revolutions, which together created a climate for any courageous individual to make a stand.

Norwich, as the 'Athens of England' and a cradle of nonconformist action, spawned a remarkable host of dissenting 'angels'. The social reformers of these turbulent times were prepared for years of struggle to achieve what most of us now accept as basic rights. To this day and far into the future, rebels with a conscience will continue to push for a more just society.

The Eastern Daily Press remains an integral part of Norfolk life

Chapter Three

WOOLLY HATS WITH A CAUSE

Woolly Hats With A Cause

REBELS FOR PEACE AND THE ENVIRONMENT

During the twentieth century the struggle for improved social conditions continued. Alongside this fight grew a concern for international stability and for the environment. The First and Second World Wars revealed the fragility of world peace and the dangers of military escalation. The Cold War engendered deep fears of nuclear attack and conflicting views on how to avoid it. Simultaneously, as man's domination of the natural world grew, so did concerns about the fate of the planet, endangered animals and the threats to the environment.

The Redcoats strike back!

As one of the most rural counties of Britain, Norfolk has nurtured those who are prepared to fight for their concerns about countryside issues. Echoing the days when the Cavaliers found themselves in the dissenting camp, Norfolk's environmental rebels are not necessarily 'greens', pacifists, non-conformists, 'lefties', anarchists and eccentrics.

On 18th February 2005, the day on which hunting was outlawed, a protest rally was held on Fakenham Racecourse. The predominantly conservative or apolitical pro-hunting Countryside Alliance supporters in Norfolk were out in force. They announced that their hunts would still meet and that they would push the rules to the limit. For instance, it was still legal to flush out a fox with dogs and then to shoot it.

The Fakenham Racecourse demonstration was part of a campaign that had already seen mass rallies in London, where the police had found themselves up against a new kind of demonstrator. As the government

A Norfolk hunt rallies

was pushing the hunting ban through Parliament, antihunt campaigners accused Henry Bellingham, Member of Parliament for North West Norfolk and Shadow Minister for Rural Affairs, of inciting pro-hunt protestors to cause obstruction with their horse boxes on the M25 motorway, and to hound and picket ministers who supported the ban! The Chief Constable of Norfolk passed the allegations on to the Metropolitan Police, who were already investigating the case of a pro-hunt group that had broken into the House of Commons. The pro-hunting lobby argues that hunting helps rural income and conservation, while those against hunting describe it as unnecessary cruelty.

From sabotage to the pen

Anti-hunt campaigners have been considered rebels for a long time, because many of them are willing to break the law in support of their beliefs. In 1999 a group of hunt saboteurs attacked some farmers and hunt foot followers at North Elmham in Norfolk, and one of the saboteurs was arrested. Many criticise the more extreme and violent tactics of animal rights people, some of which have led to imprisonment; but from the activists' point of view, animals are being tortured and murdered.

Most of those campaigning for animal rights employ more peaceful tactics. In 2003 Norwich antiblood sports supporters occupied Foxley Woods near Bawdeswell, in an attempt to stop the deer cull. Much of their work involves letters and petitions.

"No thee cruel man!"

Norfolk has a history of animal rights campaigning, particularly with regards to horses. Anna Sewell, who wrote the classic novel *Black Beauty*, was born in Great Yarmouth in 1820. Anna's family was Quaker and so compassion was embedded in her philosophy of life. Her rebellious spirit and concern for animals was evident when, as a young girl, she saw a neighbour shoot a blackbird. 'No thee cruel man, thee shan't have it at all,' she said! She could not bear to watch the suffering of horses, and during the last few years of her life in the village of Buxton, north of Norwich, she expressed her concerns in *Black Beauty*, published in 1877 by Jarrold's, the Norwich bookseller. In the novel, she revealed the horse's pain through his own eyes. George Ansell, an American who aimed to bring animal rights to public attention, printed

The plaque on Anna Sewell's Buxton home

33

the book and its popularity grew, bringing Anna's concerns to public attention. In particular she helped to put a stop to the use of the harmful bearing rein.

The maltreatment of horses was a cause taken up by another Norfolk woman, Ada Cole, who was born in 1860 at Croxton Hall Farm near Thetford. She was an unconventional character who, in later life, befriended the eccentric theosophist and vegetarian, Annie Bessant. Ada Cole's lone protests earned her the reputation of being something of a crank. She met with ridicule as she confronted the drovers at the markets around Cley-next-the-Sea, taking them to task over the transportation, in appalling conditions, of old horses to abattoirs on the continent. Despite the abuse, she stood firm. Stephen Coleridge, a barrister, who was also an animal welfare supporter and antivivisectionist, assisted her.

Ada Cole's years of campaigning finally led to the Exportation of Horses Act in 1914, the legislation that curtailed much of the cruelty to horses. Through the war years she continued to campaign, showing bravery and spirit akin to that of another courageous Norfolk woman, Nurse Edith Cavell (Chapter 7).

Working as a nurse with her sister, Ada Cole helped escapees from German-occupied Belgium. Both sisters were caught, but unlike the unfortunate Cavell who was killed by a German firing squad, she and her sister were saved by the Armistice, and freed. Back in Norfolk, Ada Cole continued to fight for better treatment of horses and was instrumental in the formation of the International League for the Protection of Horses, which campaigns to this day, now under the name of World Horse Welfare. In December 2004 it was largely responsible for the European Union decision to regulate for the transportation of animals in humane conditions.

The rebel Lord

Lord Peter Melchett: environmental warrior

A present-day campaigner with a deep concern for both animals and the environment, and close ties with Norfolk, is Lord Peter Melchett. He is not, as his title might suggest, a right-wing establishment figure, but a Labour peer and executive director of Greenpeace UK. Greenpeace is world-renowned for its bold initiatives in the face of entrenched vested interests on a range of environmental causes.

Despite his place within the English aristocracy, Peter

Melchett's protest activities have brought accusations of vandalism. Rebellion runs in the family veins. His great-grandfather and founder of ICI, Sir Alfred Mond, in protest against treatment of Jews under the Third Reich, recommended the boycott of the 1936 Berlin Olympic Games. After receiving his Labour peerage, Peter Melchett lost little time in speaking out against the cruel treatment of animals in zoos. As a young boy he had been deeply affected by the sight of hundreds of partridges dying as a result of ingesting pesticides at Courtyard Farm, his family's North Norfolk estate. This incident was a factor behind his decision to take action against genetically modified (GM) crops in a widely reported protest rally in 1999.

One morning at dawn, he and his fellow Greenpeace activists put on white 'contamination' suits and broke in through gates protecting GM crops in a farm at Lyng, near Dereham. They managed to pull up about half of the plants before the farmer alerted the police. The activists were arrested and Melchett was briefly put behind bars. In a blaze of publicity, the jury acquitted him. Subsequently, in 2000 with the Lord Mayor of Norwich he launched a campaign to turn Norfolk into a 'GM-free zone'. Practising what he preaches, Peter Melchett owns an organic farm in Norfolk, where no pesticides are used or genetically modified crops grown.

'Du different'

The trend away from conventional farming methods and conventional jobs, and into organic farming is gaining pace. David Barker from Wolterton in north Norfolk once had a professional desk job, but finds organic farming much more rewarding. He practises the 'bio-dynamic' method of organic farming, believing it to be closer to the natural system. The farming calendar, from planting through to harvesting, is guided by the stars and involves the use of herbal preparations to enhance earth forces and silicon for light

David Barker (left) at his bio-dynamic farm at Wolterton

energy. David proudly states in the magazine *Eco Echo* that the Norfolk motto is 'Du Different'!

From the 'Battle for the Broads' to the 'Dirty Dozen'

Another Norfolk man who set out to 'du different' by making a positive mark on the environment was Andrew Lees, born in 1949 in Great Yarmouth. He achieved much success in his work for Friends of the Earth before his death at age 46 in Madagascar, while campaigning to stop a proposed titanium mine.

Described both as obsessive and inspirational, Andrew Lees once explained to a friend that he believed in giving oneself over totally to a cause. He lived by his creed, uncompromisingly making his mark in a push for a more environmentally-safe world. Lees began his career as a scientist, later drawing on his scientific knowledge and analytical mind to become an influential full time activist. In 1982 he was a leading force behind the creation of Broadlands Friends of the Earth, in a battle to save the Norfolk Broads from drainage that would create fields for cereals and destroy the unique natural ecosystem. This 'Battle for the Broads' saved huge areas of wetlands when, in 1988, the Norfolk and Suffolk Broads Act was passed through Parliament. Andrew went on to become the Friends of the Earth campaign officer for pesticides and the countryside, and for toxins and pollution. He exposed a Norfolk chemicals manufacturer for unlawful effluents, and his 'Dirty Dozen' campaign succeeded in controlling and banning a number of toxic chemicals.

Lees was not intimidated by power. He did not hesitate to go over the head of the British Government to appeal to the European Union. It was partly due to his campaign that the Government finally tightened controls on water quality. He was prepared to

Andrew Lees fought to save the beautiful Norfolk Broads

brave dangerous conditions too. On a mission to Nigeria, he exposed the dumping of 8,000 tonnes of toxic waste, most of it from Italy, and tracked it to the Karin B cargo ship.

Appointed Friends of the Earth's national campaigns director, Lees continued to fight with a dedicated passion for the causes he believed in until his death. While on assignment in Madagascar, he continued working in spite of ill health. He died of heat stroke while alone in the forest shooting a final piece of film for his latest project. Andrew Lees is nationally admired for his courage, tenacity and deeply held principles. The Andrew Lees Trust was set up in his honour to support the causes closest to his heart: the environment and people of Madagascar.

For peace, the land and beyond... going for it!

Yet another dynamic and controversial environmental figure in the environmental

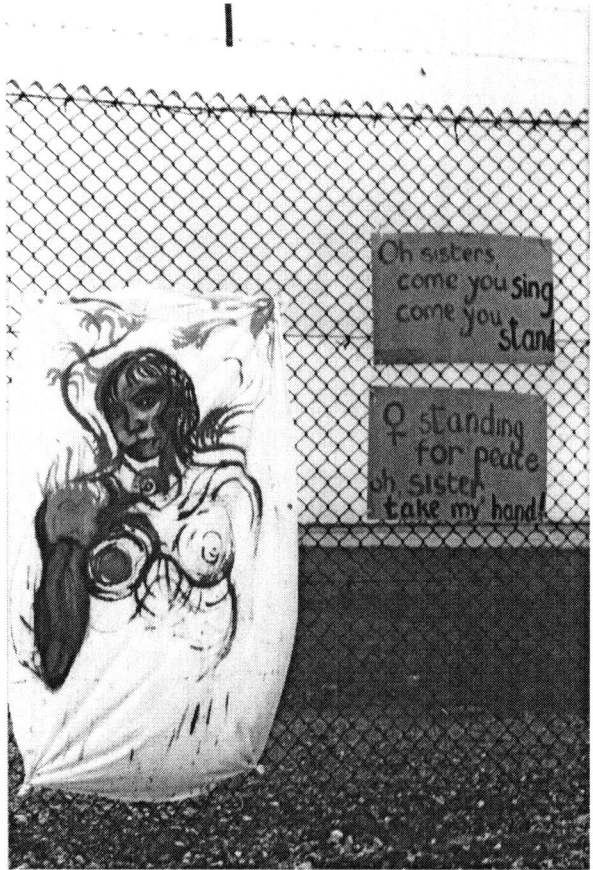

Protest at Greenham Common

field is Norfolk-based campaigner Angie Zelter. Zelter was also a passionate advocate for world peace, and a CND supporter. Her involvement with the Peace Movement developed in the late 1970s and in 1980 she started the Snowball Campaign to protest against nuclear weapons by cutting the perimeter wires of nuclear airbases. Close to 2,800 campaigners were arrested.

Zelter was jailed for two months in Malaysia for campaigning against Sarawak's export of timber. She remained undaunted and continued to campaign against rainforest destruction both in England and abroad. She ran the UK Forest Network and created the North Norfolk Community Woodland Trust, which bought land and established a public woodland near North Walsham.

Again in rebellious mode, she helped to damage a Hawk jet, which she believed to be illegally bound for East Timor to assist in the murder of the island's citizens. In Scotland, with two other women campaigners, she threw equipment into a loch while breaking into Faslane naval base, intent on stopping the illegal use of nuclear weapons. All three women spent five months on remand in prison, but were acquitted on the grounds that they were preventing nuclear crime. Her success in this encouraged Zelter to set up the anti nuclear weapons Trident Ploughshares project.

Angie Zelter's fight for peace went beyond protests against nuclear weapons. Concerned about the Israeli-Palestinian conflict, she helped to create the International Women's Peace Service - Palestine. This group was designed to be a monitoring presence on the West Bank of the River Jordan, seeking to stop Israeli soldiers from either harassing Palestinians or obstructing ambulances and vehicles carrying essential food and medical supplies to the communities. In Tel Aviv, she tried to expose a man who she claimed had been throwing stones at Palestinians, injuring one of them. Accused by a judge of being disruptive, in spite of the support of Israeli peace activists she was deported from Israel in January 2003.

Her spirit unbroken, within a month she and a group of women who were allied to an organisation called Women in Black attempted to enter the House of Commons to protest against the imminent invasion of Iraq. Her peace activities continued into 2006, when she was arrested for illegally boarding a military aircraft to investigate the transportation

Norwich prison: 'home' to a succession of rebels!

of arms to Israel.

Angie Zelter is a controversial figure and most certainly a Norfolk rebel. She is a woman of enormous courage and resilience, and is prepared to put herself in danger and to suffer for her beliefs.

A number of peace groups in Norfolk have been involved with the campaign against the US-led operation in Iraq and have organised demonstrations and vigils. Individuals and groups who make a stand against war are often labelled unpatriotic and criticised on the basis that failure to take action would allow the enemy in. But pacifists argue that violence engenders more violence. In the First and Second World Wars, radical thinkers like Dorothy Jewson and Henry Massingham made such beliefs known, and the Quakers followed their own traditional belief in non-violence.

A question of morals

Frank Nolan, a Quaker resident of Aylsham in North Norfolk, was a conscientious objector in the Second World War. His father had been in the army since age 14, and his father's friends made their disapproval clear. Having registered as a conscientious objector just before the start of the war when living in Cambridge, Nolan had to appear before a tribunal. He left no doubt as to his position, stating that war was against his ethics, and questioning how it could be possible to go to war while also loving our enemies. He believed that war engenders fear and hatred. His objection was to killing for his country, not to dying for it. He must have argued eloquently, for he received exemption. He had known that if the tribunal decided to reject his request not to go to war he could have faced imprisonment. Many of those who stood before the tribunal as conscientious objectors a few months later were turned down, including a friend of Nolan, who received a gaol sentence.

People who campaign on issues like peace or the environment are characterised by many as the naïve 'woolly hat' brigade, or labelled disruptive and dangerous. Their beliefs often run counter to government policy, the concerns of big business or fears for national safety. Some people are rebellious by nature and a few employ violent tactics, but irrespective of the right or wrong of their cause, most campaigners have genuine concerns. In a world where wars are always present and peace seems fragile, and where we see alarming signs of pending environmental disaster, this should not be surprising.

The School of Environmental Studies at UEA in Norwich has taken a lead in groundbreaking research on climate change, marking the point where environmental rebels and serious scientists concur. The work of environmentalists like Andrew Lees combined with leading academic institutions like UEA

led governments to establish the Kyoto Protocol, which aims to cut the greenhouse gasses that cause global warming.

Norfolk campaigners have made valuable contributions to geo-political and environmental issues, challenging policies and practices at all levels of society, at home and around the world.

Chapter Four

MARTYRS, HERETICS & SCAPEGOATS

Martyrs, Heretics & Scapegoats

A FIGHT FOR SPIRITUAL FREEDOM

Norfolk's history shows just how much oppression has both stifled and encouraged religious rebellion. The struggle for spiritual freedom and release from the established church's stranglehold was particularly powerful in Norfolk. It demanded unusually brave or foolhardy rebels to confront the strength and aggression of the establishment.

By the end of the thirteenth century, bolstered by the financial rewards of the Crusades and a lucrative relic business, the Roman Catholic Church in England had grown enormously wealthy. People resented it both for its riches and for the crippling tolls it placed on trades people.

The Prior's men in arms and the Tombland Riot

Norwich citizens were often at loggerheads with the monastery that lay close by the cathedral. The townspeople had attacked the monastery in 1234, but a particularly bloody confrontation occurred in 1272, later known as the Tombland Riot. William de Burnham, the prior, and his band of sword-wielding men, took action after a series of disturbances created by the townspeople. The prior's men fired on citizens in the Norwich streets and went on to raid and pillage a merchant's house and a tavern, where they also

Tombland Alley, Ethelbert Gate, Bishop's Palace Gate and Cathdral Gate, witness to many bloody scenes

had their fill of wine!

The direct aggression, coming on top of the prohibitive tolls, was too much for the townspeople, who fought back for three days. They broke into the cathedral precinct, set fire to buildings, damaged the cathedral itself and killed some of the monks. The retribution was heavy. Henry III himself presided over the trial and 30 Norwich citizens were sent to execution. Some were hung, drawn and quartered, while others were dragged by horses around the streets until they were dead. One woman was burned alive for having set fire to the cathedral gates. Those whose lives were spared were forced to build St. Ethelbert Gateway, which still stands today as a reminder of the rebellion. The bishop imprisoned the prior but the monks escaped punishment.

Tensions between church and people continued to grow. By the 1370s, when the cost of the French war was becoming onerous, even the House of Commons was asking for Papal taxation to be lifted, and began to resent the Church's wealth. The 1381 Peasants' Revolt arose largely from this hatred of the Church, and resulted in the murder of Archbishop Sudbury of Canterbury. His head was paraded on a spike through the London streets, and today his skull is kept inside St. Gregory's and St. Peter's Church in Sudbury, his home town in Suffolk. In Norfolk Bishop Despenser of Norwich used his military might to quell Litester's rebellion (Chapter 1).

Tyranny of the bishops and the evil pit

Bishop Despenser had a particular loathing of the Lollards, a group of Christians who rebelled against the Church. They were inspired by the writings of John Wycliffe (1330-1384), a doctor of divinity at Oxford University who completed the first English translation of the Bible. Wycliffe also questioned church hierarchy, Papal power and Catholic doctrine. When Henry IV came to power in 1399 he put the Lollards into the Church's hands, much to satisfaction of Bishop Despenser. Soon after, at a trial presided over by Despenser, William Sawtre became the first Lollard to be burned in England; he was executed at Smithfield in 1401. Sawtre, a priest of St. Margarets, Lynn, had earlier recanted but was again caught preaching and consigned into Despenser's hands.

In the late 1420s Bishop William Alnwick of Norwich

Bishopsbridge, where many grisly procession has advanced

The Bridge House, once a women's prison

followed in Despenser's footsteps by trying to purge the Lollards. It was at this time that the infamous Lollards' Pit, a chalk pit near Bishopsbridge in Norwich, was chosen for the site of execution. The large crowd it attracted watched with ghoulish fascination as the victim's flesh burned away and the bones began to fall into the ashes below. It is not surprising that the Lollards' Pit was later avoided as a place of evil. In the words of George Henry Borrow (Chapter 7), "many a saint of God has breathed his last breath beneath that white precipice, midst flame and pitch; many grisly procession has advanced... across the old bridge towards the Lollards hole..." Even today nobody lives on that spot. It is the site of a large gas-holder close to the Bridgehouse pub, once a women's prison, which bears a plaque in remembrance of the Lollards Pit victims.

In 1428 William White and two others were the first victims to be burned to death in the Lollards' Pit. White stood against idolatry, the Pope and the Catholic Church. Like Sawtre, he had recanted but was arrested a second time for preaching in the streets. When he refused again to recant, he was brought before the Bishop of Norwich. He was forced to carry the kindling wood for his own execution fire. As he walked towards the pit, he continued to preach until he was hit on the mouth, pelted with missiles and covered with the excrement of chamber pots.

In contrast to the cruel lack of respect the people of Norwich showed White in 1428, they were full of concern for Thomas Bilney when he was taken to the same fate in the

Lollards Pit, 'a place of evil'

Lollards' Pit in 1531. In the hundred years following White's execution, public resentment had continued to grow and subtle changes were taking place. The influence of Martin Luther, a self-confessed supporter of Wycliffe's ideas who initiated the German Reformation in 1517, was growing. Only five years later, public sentiment against the church allowed Henry VIII to dissolve the monasteries.

Despite public sympathy and although he questioned only a few aspects of the Catholic faith, Bilney suffered the same grisly death in the Lollards' Pit. He was a friend of Bishop Hugh Latimer, who was also executed, and of Matthew Parker (Chapter 9), whose highly placed connections were unable to protect Bilney from his cruel fate. Cardinal Wolsey and other churchmen convicted him of heresy. He recanted, but he was later caught preaching again. Following his arrest on the orders of Bishop Richard Nix of Norwich, several monks gave evidence against him. As he burned at the stake, the outpouring of public sympathy for Bilney gave cause for the church to worry that people might withhold alms, even though Bilney told the crowd not to blame the monks, because it was "God's will". He was a man of deep faith: the night before his execution he had put a finger into a flame and said that he looked forward to the joy of the afterlife.

Bilney's endurance was put to the test at the stake, the flames blowing in various directions and prolonging his agony before extinguishing his life.

After Bilney, the worst burnings occurred between 1553 and 1558 under the rule of the Catholic "Bloody Mary" and the supervision of John Hopton, another merciless Bishop of Norwich who had been Mary's confessor before she became Queen. Canterbury and London excepted, more people were burnt in Norwich than any other city. Norwich Cathedral records list 170 executions by fire during this period, mainly of Protestants.

Newcomers and new ideas

During the reign of Elizabeth I, the Protestant and Puritan movements grew. They were strengthened further by the arrival refugees from the Low Country, who followed the beliefs of the French Protestant, John Calvin (1509-1564). These people had been severely persecuted by the Catholic ruler, Philip of Spain. In 1565 Norwich gained permission from the Crown to take in a number of Dutch, Flemish and Walloon families to help boost the City's textile industry. So Norwich became a haven for persecuted rebels instead of being their repressor! Strangers Hall was their first home. Although they had been invited to Norwich, the city's citizens viewed them as competition for work. In 1570 a group of townspeople hatched a plan to rid the city of the 'strangers' and to bring down Elizabeth's essentially Protestant government. Ironically, Thomas Kett, who was a conspirator and a relation of the famous rebel Robert Kett, exposed the plot. The conspirators were caught and three men were executed.

Now that Catholic power had diminished, many people were inspired by reformation ideas and were encouraged by the Low Country immigrants. The Family of Love sect, which believed in peaceful communal living and a direct relationship with God, developed

*Strangers' Hall, home to persecuted rebels
from abroad in the 16th century*

from Dutch Anabaptist ideas and was active in Norfolk.

Robert Browne (1550-1633) became the leader of the Brownists. He had been attracted by the religious freedom of Norwich, where the Low Country refugees were encouraging a strong Puritan influence. But the Norwich authorities were not as broad minded as he had hoped. A rebel critical of both Church and Government, Browne soon lost the support of Bishop Edmund Freak of Norwich. With his Norwich friend Robert Harrison and other followers, Browne fled to Holland and began to publish books.

On his return to England, he was excommunicated and imprisoned but later made peace with the Church. His followers in Norwich were not so lucky. Those who distributed his writings were hanged.

There were other victims of the establishment's prejudice. Norwich priest Theopholis Brabourne (1590-1662) was thrown into a parliamentary gaol for supporting Sabbatarian ideas (observing Saturday, the Jewish Sabbath). It was still a dangerous time for non-conformists. However, the tide was turning and as the English Civil War began, the Puritan rebels were poised for revenge.

Pillaging and drinking in the cathedral

In 1642 the oppressive Bishop Wren (uncle of Sir Christopher Wren), who had been particularly harsh on foreigners, was imprisoned in the Tower of London along with the more moderate Joseph Hall, who subsequently succeeded Wren as bishop of Norwich.

The following year bishops were declared delinquents and deprived of much of their money. At the same time, the Norwich Puritans decided to rebel in style: they smashed the windows and organ pipes of the cathedral and all symbols of what they called idolatry were burnt on a great bonfire in the market place.

Signs of the rebellion remain in the cathedral today: parliamentary musketeers' graffiti, missing heads of statues and a musket ball still embedded in Bishop Goldwell's tomb. Bishop Hall described the cathedral's desicration as "drinking and tobacconing as freely as if it had turned alehouse". In 1650 the Puritan authorities at Great Yarmouth petitioned Parliament to use materials from what they referred to as the 'vast' and 'useless' cathedral, to build a workhouse for the poor and to repair the Yarmouth piers! The request was refused and the cathedral was refurbished.

'The Big Blow'

Although Norfolk had a Puritan bias during the Civil War, there was a backlash when the influence became too oppressive. In Norwich in 1647, the rebels suddenly lent their support to their erstwhile opponents. The moderate mayor, John Utting, disregarded Puritan pressure to crush all old church traditions. The local Puritans complained to Parliament, which despatched the former mayor to take Utting into

The magnificent west facade of Norwich Cathedral

custody. The rebellious Norwich population was once again in action! Apprentices, other townspeople and Royalists rioted in support of Utting. One account describes a rioter wielding a pitchfork and shouting, "... take them alive – now for these roundheadly rogues and whores"! They attacked and raided the Puritan aldermen's houses and confronted the East Dereham cavalry with the arms the East Dereham cavalry with the arms they had just stolen. An oil lamp was knocked over and ignited gunpowder, blowing up the Committee House and killing several people. A saddler, Henry Goward, was condemned as a ringleader and hanged with seven others on the Castle Ditches in 1649. John Utting was fined and imprisoned.

Hundreds of years of Catholic repression had produced an extreme reaction, which in its turn encouraged counter-rebellion in the most moderate of citizens. Many clergy were ejected for their Royalist or 'popish' sympathies. Nethaniel Gill, a moderate rector of Burgh-next-Aylsham in north Norfolk was sequestered, but he defiantly continued his church work with the support of his congregation. It took the authorities years to catch up with him, and when they did in 1651 he was promptly sent to Bungay to retire. But come the Restoration in 1660, he returned to Burgh as rector. A more attractive target for the prim Puritans was the rector of Earsham, Nicholas Sherwood, who was accused of incontinency, being an 'alehouse haunter', a 'gamester' and a 'swearer'!

Intrigue, treason and plot

Many of the Catholic hunters were now the hunted. This turning of the tables had begun with Henry VIII's break with Rome in the 1530s, and escalated after the Protestant Elizabeth ascended the throne in 1558. Those Catholics who had been all-powerful establishment figures were now viewed as heretics and rebels. One such character was Thomas Howard, fourth Duke of Norfolk (from 1554 to 1572). He was a large Norfolk landowner, with a mansion at Kenninghall and a palace in Norwich that was regarded as one of the most beautiful homes in England. The site in Duke Street is now a multi-story car park! Thomas's father, Henry, Earl of Surrey and cousin to both Catherine Howard and Anne Boleyn, was the last person to be executed under Henry VIII, sentenced on suspicion of Catholicism and of intrigue against the crown. Thomas Howard was imprisoned for secretly negotiating to marry the Catholic Mary, Queen of Scots. Then, in 1570 he was drawn into the Ridolfi Plot, a plan to assassinate Queen Elizabeth and crown Mary, enabling Philip of Spain to invade England. The plot was discovered, Thomas Howard was tried for treason and executed in 1572.

Traitors Gate, through which prisoners passed into the Tower of London

Outlawed priests and Catholic noblemen

Some people chose to defy the Protestants by converting to Catholicism. In an ironic twist of fate, one such man, Robert Southwell (1561-1595), was the grandson of Richard Southwell, who had brought Thomas Howard's father, Henry, to his execution.

Robert Southwell was born at Horsham St. Faith's in Norfolk. Intrigued by Catholicism, he rebelled against his family's protestant beliefs, becoming a Jesuit priest in 1584. As a missionary he defied the law that forbade English Catholic priests to be in England for more than 40 days at a time. Under the name of Cotton and in disguise, he preached in secret but was eventually caught, tortured and imprisoned for three years. Incarcerated in prison he turned to writing poetry, which is believed to have influenced William Shakespeare. A victim of circumstance, Southwell was hanged and quartered for treason at Tyburn in London in 1595. At this time rumours of Catholic plots were rife, and punishments were harsh.

It was hard for Catholic priests to go unnoticed; the danger of being revealed to the authorities was ever-present. At the time of the Civil War a priest, Thomas Tunstal, managed to escape imprisonment by climbing down a rope from Wisbech Castle. He made for a Royalist's family's house near King's Lynn. The inhabitants sought the help of Lady L'Estrange to tend his wounds. Unfortunately for Tunstal, Lady L'Estrange's husband Sir Harmon was an Anglican, even though he was a Royalist. He ordered the priest's capture. Tunstal was tried in Norwich Castle and condemned to death.

Outlawed priests and other Catholics were often forced to conceal themselves. Nicholas Owen, an English Jesuit who landed in Norfolk on his return from abroad, was a saviour to these 'outlaws'. He managed to build many ingeniously concealed hiding

Oxborough Hall

places, known as priest holes, before being arrested, tortured and executed in the Tower of London. One priest hole was at Oxburgh, Norfolk, home to the Catholic Bedingfeld family. Sir Henry Bedingfeld (1509-1583) was instrumental in the crowning of Mary Tudor. Under Elizabeth's rule, because he refused to go to the local church, he was repeatedly fined and prohibited from travelling more than five miles from his home without official permission. The Bedingfelds were penalised further during the Civil War. The Sir Henry of that era was imprisoned in the Tower. Oxburgh was occupied and during this period suffered damage by fire.

Norfolk's Jacobite

Following the Restoration of 1660 and the crowning of Charles II there was a backlash against Puritanism and renewed persecution of non-conformists. In 1662, the Act of Uniformity forced two thousand so-called non-conformist rectors out of their parishes. This return to Royalist conservatism increased fears that Catholicism might again take hold. In 1688, there were anti-Catholic riots. A mob pillaged Catholic dwellings and destroyed the Catholic chapel in Blackfriar's Yard in Norwich.

1688 was also the year that the Catholic monarch James Stuart was removed from the throne, and his supporters, who became known as Jacobites, set about re-instating him. Christopher Layer, a wealthy barrister from Booton near Aylsham in Norfolk was, like many Jacobites, unpopular. He went to Rome to speak to James Stuart's son, later known as James 'The Pretender'. Layer came back to England with plans for a return of the House of Stuart. He sought to raise an army, but he was under suspicion and was arrested. After a failed attempt to escape across the Thames from Whitehall he admitted his plot to bring about a coup d'etat, but he did not reveal details of his co-conspirators, even though he had been betrayed by some of them. In 1723 he was hung, drawn and quartered at Tyburn, and his head was placed on a pole for all to

Christopher Layer's home, now Barclays Bank

50

see. Today a commemorative plaque is on a wall of his home in Aylsham, now the Aylsham branch of Barclays Bank. An Indian prince, in exile in Norfolk, placed it there in 1908.

Non-conformists v. the Hellfire Club!

It was not until the passing of the 1689 Toleration Act that both non-conformists and Catholics were able to openly observe their faith and persuasion without official hindrance. In the preceding years the Quakers had held their meetings in Norwich gaol for convenience, as so many of them were imprisoned there! Liberated by the Toleration Act, the Quakers built the Old Meeting House in Colegate, Norwich. Nonconformists gained in strength, particularly among artisans and intellectuals.

But rebellion came from a new quarter. A group of young upper class men, calling themselves the Hellfire Club and widely regarded as a hooligan bunch, had a penchant for debauched drinking. They harboured a particular hatred of the pious John Wesley and his Methodist followers. The Hellfire Club would gather at the Bell Hotel in Norwich and make plans to attack the Methodists. Tanked up with alcohol, they attacked John Wesley and his brother Charles when they visited Norwich in 1754. They paid bands of armed face-blackened rioters and plied them with drink. One of these mobs staged a mock funeral procession for 'Hell-fire Dick' outside the house of a preacher they deplored and then burned the coffin in the castle ditches.

Flying in the face of tradition

During the eighteenth and nineteenth centuries, a number of non-conformists rebelled against society. Many Norwich Quakers, including Elizabeth Fry (Chapter 2), were increasingly vocal in their demands for social improvements. The Unitarians pushed for social reform and strongly challenged Christian thinking. Opposed to dogma in all its forms, they denied the immaculate conception and believed Jesus to have been an ordinary man.

Harriet Martineau (1802-1876) was a Norwich Unitarian (Chapter

The Bell Hotel: favoured haunt of The Hellfire Club

Octagon Chapel, Quakers Hall

5), who took the move away from traditional thinking even further. Her lineage and personal development followed an interesting, sometimes rebellious path. Her family were French Huguenots, a group of Calvinists who had come to England to escape persecution about a hundred years after the Low Country Calvinists. Martineau's parents and brother James were strict Unitarians, but her enquiring mind led her towards mesmerism, clairvoyance and a tendency towards philosophical atheism. When in 1851 these views were exposed in her book *Letters on the Laws of Man's Nature and Development*, she was flying in the face of her family's Unitarian beliefs; the relationship between her and her brother James was damaged irreparably.

With the majority of church schools in the hands of the Anglican church in 1904, many nonconformists, including the Primitive Methodists of Aldborough, refused to pay that part of the poor rate which supported education. Their property was seized. Some Quakers were penalised for refusing to fight in the two World Wars (Chapter 3), but generally religious discrimination lessened during the twentieth century. An influx of ethnic groups with their cultures and religions into large towns like Norwich brought increasing religious diversity and acceptance.

Accusations of ritual murder

One thousand years ago It was a different story for foreign immigrants. Christians unwilling to conform to the state's brand of Christianity were not the only people to suffer persecution. In the years following the Norman Conquest, a Jewish community developed in Norwich. Until 1159 it accounted for seven percent of the city's population. The Jews became the focus for jealousy and resentment, partly because people were in their debt (ironically, Jewish money helped to fund the building of Norwich Cathedral), but also because of their 'foreign' way of life and religion, which did not conform to Christian dogma and English culture.

The first ritual murder charge against the Jews, which set off a host of similar

52

accusations in other countries and which, hundreds of years later, added fuel to Hitler's cruel damnation of the Jews, was in Norwich in 1144. Twelve-year-old William was found dead in a wood. His uncle, a priest named Godwin Sturt, accused the Jews of murder. Monk Thomas of Monmouth called William a martyr and fabricated a story that the Jews had ritually sacrificed the boy at Easter as a mockery of Christ's Passion. Lack of evidence meant that no Jews were executed but a number were unlawfully killed.

The Crusaders particularly hated the Jews, likening them to Muslims because of their different religion and place of origin. In 1190 Crusaders killed Jews and burned their houses in the Port of Lynn. Norwich Jews took refuge in the castle, under Royal protection. That protection ended in 1290 when King Edward I ordered all Jews in England, under pain of death, to leave the country. This was the same year that the long-running Crusades failed. Crusaders had announced that their time would be better spent dealing with the Jews at home than with fighting 'infidels' in the Holy Land. It was not until 1656 that Cromwell lifted the ban and some Jews began to come to England. However, as with the non-conformists and Catholics, official discrimination continued for a further 200 years. A Jewish community began to develop and thrive in Norwich from the mid nineteenth century.

Hunting down 'witches'

Things supernatural or beyond the bounds of Church belief were treated with suspicion for many hundreds of years in Europe. Even women who were unconventional, alone, ugly, owners of house pets, retarded, malformed, disabled, or good with herbs or midwifery, were accused of witchcraft. In 1484 when Pope Innocent VIII declared that the devil worked through his minions, major witch-hunts were precipitated in Germany, France and Scotland. In the sixteenth and early seventeenth centuries laws against witchcraft were passed, but old superstitions lingered.

In 1583 'Old Mother Gabley' of King's Lynn was accused of causing a shipwreck by placing eggs in water; because the eggs

The Tolhouse, Yarmouth, where 'witches' were kept the night before execution

floated, she was tried and duly executed! Two out of the three recorded English 'witch' burnings were in Norfolk. In 1590 Margaret Read of King's Lynn was accused of using witchcraft to kill her husband. Her heart is said to have exploded from her body as she burned at the stake, and the place where it came to rest is marked by a heart shape on a house in Tuesday Market Place. In 1659 Mary Oliver, also believed to have bewitched her husband to death, was burned in Norwich.

In 1603 James I had inflamed the situation by encouraging witch-hunting. The problem reached a peak in East Anglia in 1645 when Matthew Hopkins, the 'Witchfinder General' from Manningtree began to roam the area. To test some victims, he dunked them in water and found them guilty if they floated! Through sleep depravation, solitary confinement and starvation he forced confessions out of suspected witches, asking people to come forward with grievances to make each case. Hopkins toured Essex and Suffolk, before moving on to Norfolk, accusing 'witches' in King's Lynn, Norwich and Great Yarmouth. At least five so-called witches were hanged in Yarmouth following his investigations in 1645. They were mostly elderly spinsters and widows, including Elizabeth Bradwell who was accused of putting a spell on a local boy who had died.

Hopkins earned good money from his infamous activities and started to target wealthier citizens.   But the people began to turn on him and Parliament questioned the witchfinder's tactics. One report suggests that he died in 1648 of consumption, but another says that he himself was accused of witchcraft and was either hanged or drowned by water-dunking. In the 1960s a Vincent Price movie, *The Witchfinder General* told Hopkins' story, bringing the horror of his barbaric campaign to contemporary audiences.

During the Restoration, witch hunting became less common. The Witchcraft Act of 1736, while abolishing the death penalty for witches, nevertheless laid down punishments for those caught calling up spirits or casting spells. Clairvoyant readings, pagan meetings and spiritualist events grew in popularity as the authorities increasingly turned a 'blind eye', but prejudice remained. As late as 1835, when Frances Billings and Catherine Fray were executed for murder in Norwich, reports suggested that they had consulted 'reputed witches'.

The confusion of attitudes is shown in a story concerning Queen Victoria's son, the Prince of Wales.   When he bought the Sandringham estate in Norfolk in 1853, 'wise' women were evicted from the estate cottages, but the agent was so afraid of the reputed powers of one that he let her stay. When the Prince of Wales fell ill in 1880, he allowed this woman to give him mandrake wine to cure him.

As late as the Second World War, a clairvoyant was imprisoned for fear that she would reveal evidence of plans for D-Day. Under pressure from spiritualists, the Witchcraft Act was finally repealed in 1951. In 2001 on the fiftieth anniversary of that repeal a celebration was held at the Assembly House in Norwich and the Norwich moot was invited to join the Norwich Inter Faith Link. Pagans, including those who called themselves 'witches', were recognised as part of a multi-faceted spiritual community.

Full circle to a pagan past

A recent cause for spiritual rebellion in Norfolk had its origin in pre-history. A circle of wooden posts around an up-turned tree trunk in the sea (near Holme-next-the-Sea), probably once used for ritual purposes and referred to as 'Seahenge', became a *cause celebre*. In May 1999 English Heritage decided to remove Seahenge, claiming that seawater was eroding it. Druids, including Archdruid of

The ancient Seahenge

Stonehenge Rollo Maughfling, joined in protest with spiritual healer and painter Sam Jones and conservationist Buster Nolan, and other environmental campaigners, pagans, local Holme residents and concerned public.

They objected to the proposed removal as vandalism and sacrilege. The Druids and other pagans believed Seahenge to be cited on an ancient sacred spot. Peaceful protest held up much of the excavation, and when a meeting was arranged between protesters and English Heritage, no agreement was reached. The protestors felt cheated. Soon afterwards, Rollo Maughfling stood on the central oak and declared that removing Seahenge would be tantamount to moving Stonehenge or Canterbury Cathedral. English Heritage took out an injunction to stop protesters from obstructing their work, but local businessman Mervyn Lambert supported the protestors' cause. Finally, the Royal High Court of Justice decided that English Heritage should in future show more consideration for local spiritual concerns, but the court allowed the excavation to continue. The 'rebels' put up an effective fight, but the establishment ultimately gained the upper hand.

A spiritual paradox

Over the years, spiritual rebellion has been strong in Norfolk, and the response was swift and repressive. The Norfolk authorities were responsible for the first Lollard to be burned in England, the first accusation of Jewish ritual murder, and two of three witch burnings in the country.

At the same time, Norwich is the only city in England to name a street 'Synagogue Street', reflecting a thriving Jewish community. The intellectual and creative communities of Norfolk encouraged the emergence of radical religious ideas. Many nonconformist movements were either born or nurtured in Norfolk, and they were strongly influenced by the persecuted Calvinist families who made Norwich home. Norfolk has welcomed new people and nurtured spiritual beliefs for centuries, while also persecuting them.

Chapter Five

OVER DEVOUT, OVER SEXED, OVER THERE AND OVER HERE!

Over Devout, Over Sexed, Over There & Over Here!

THE NORFOLK & AMERICA CONUNDRUM

There have been many links between Norfolk and America over the years. The evidence remains today in the number of places named after Norfolk and its towns, villages and rivers – especially in the state of Virginia and elsewhere on the Eastern seaboard of the United States. It is believed that Captain Adam Thorowgood (1604-1640), a native of King's Lynn, named the town of Norfolk, Virginia, and the Lynnhaven River.

Heacham, John Rolf's home village

Why did so many Norfolk people head west across the Atlantic? Influenced by its close links with the sea, Norfolk has been home to a number of merchants and seafaring adventurers and many dissatisfied and persecuted nonconformists (Chapter 4).

Many of the early immigrants to America – the New World – had good reason to reject the 'Old World' and were of rebellious spirit. Even those who went to America on mercantile missions sometimes stayed on, lured into a wild world so different from the relatively tame one they had left behind.

A Norfolk entrepreneur and a heathen princess

John Rolf was typical of those who stayed. A wealthy man from Heacham Hall in Norfolk, he became an early settler. In 1610 he and his wife had landed in Virginia to come to the aid of the Virginia Company, set up by Sir Walter Raleigh in the sixteenth century. Within months his wife died. He met and fell in love with Pocahontas, who had been kidnapped by settlers seeking to hold her father to ransom.

Pocahontas was a fun-loving indigenous Powhatan girl, who is said to have cartwheeled naked in the marketplace! She was a rebel who risked her life by literally standing in the way to stop her father, Chief Powhatan, from executing the English Captain John Smith. The English settlers were at war with the Powhatans, and John Rolf now found himself a rebel against his own people. The Powhatans were regarded as inferior and 'heathen'. Ralph Hamor, a London merchant tailor's son, wrote of Pocahontas as 'one of rude education, manners barbarous and cursed generation'. Nevertheless, Rolf wrote to Governor Dale, asking permission to marry this 'unbelieving creaure'... 'to whom my heartie and best thoughts are, and have a long time bin so entangled'. He married Pocahontas and in doing so brought eight years of peace with her tribe.

Rolf took Pocahontas and their baby son Thomas back to England. Captain John Smith wrote to Queen Anne imploring her not to be prejudiced against Pocahontas and John Rolf presented her as a foreign princess. There was disapproval, but people were nonetheless intrigued!

Pocahontas died of smallpox only a few months later at Gravesend while waiting for a boat to return to Virginia. Rolf returned to Virginia alone. Pocahontas was popularised in a Disney cartoon bearing her name, but the story bears little relationship to history.

The enterprising John Rolf introduced a successful variety of tobacco to the Virginia soil, thus saving the failing Virginia Company which went from strength to strength and enabled new pioneers, such as those on the *Mayflower* in 1620, to settle in the area.

Voyage of the pilgrims

More than half of those sailing out of Plymouth on the Mayflower were Puritan pilgrims, intent on finding religious freedom in a new land. Many had initially fled to Leiden in Holland, after King James declared: 'I will make them conform or I will harry them out of the land', while also introducing laws to force people to conform to the Anglican Church.

After a few years, anxious to retain their identity and in fear of imminent Spanish interference, the Leiden pilgrims joined other pilgrims and merchants from England for the Mayflower voyage. Some were Norfolk people. One passenger, Edward Fuller of Redenhall, had according to judicial documents been in Leiden with his family. The journey was arduous and stormy; many died before the ship finally anchored at Cape Cod.

The pilgrims settled at an abandoned Indian site, which had

The Mayflower

been named Plymouth. Almost half, including Edward Fuller, died that winter of 'The Great Sickness' though Edward's son Samuel lived to have nine children. Conditions were harsh, but the survivors were intent on building their New World and they were aided in this by an Indian chief, Massasoit. The remains of those who died are marked by a marble sarcophagus situated near a statue of Massasoit overlooking Plymouth Harbour.

'The Great Migration'

The *Mayflower* voyage marked the beginning of what came to be known as 'The Great Migration' which continued until 1643, the point at which Puritans in England began to gain the upper hand in the Civil War. Many of those who fled England at this time were from the Eastern Counties, where the repression of Puritans was particularly harsh.

In 1630 a fleet of eleven ships, known as the Winthrop Fleet after the Reverend John Winthrop, a Suffolk man who became governor of Massachusetts, left for the New World. A number of Norfolk people joined that fleet, including Reverend George Phillips, originally from Rainham St Martins, near Rougham. Phillips had studied at Cambridge University but as a nonconformist minister in Suffolk, became a victim of persecution. He and his family joined John Winthrop on the *Arbella* ship, which sailed to Salem.

The small settlement of Salem was surrounded by a dense forest that helped feed the fears and superstitions of its inhabitants in the years to come. The forest provided little room for crops and winter was looming when the settlers arrived. Harsh times called for swift measures and the community soon moved to the area now known as Boston.

George Phillips became a popuar minister of Watertown. However, as the earliest advocate of Congregationalism, his views attracted suspicion and some considered them extreme. Phillips became involved with an anti-tax protest in Watertown, eventually leading to the creation of a Massachusetts representative government. He was a rebel who found himself much more influential in his newly adopted home than in England. He had a significant impact on America's early development.

The 'Animal Farm' syndrome

In the spirit of John Winthrop's ideal of America as the 'city upon the hill' free from the repression of the English Church, many of these early pioneers set out to create a new utopia. But, in the manner of Orwell's *Animal Farm*, the other side of the story soon became apparent.

In 1640 the English settlers, who had already usurped most of the land from the native Indians, passed laws to force the Indians to convert to Christianity. It is ironic that the very pilgrims that had come to the New World as a result of persecution in Europe became instrumental in one of the most infamous 'witch trials' of history.

The East Anglian Fiske family had been zealous supporters of the Protestant Reformation for many years. Reverend John Fiske's great grandfather had escaped

Queen Mary's oppressive reign, and his great grandmother's sister had narrowly escaped execution when imprisoned in Norwich Castle. In 1637 persecution forced John Fiske to leave his ministry in Suffolk and, in disguise, he fled England with his family, making a fresh start in New England.

John Fiske's wife came from Norfolk. His brother William later married a Norfolk girl in Salem, and William's daughter married a Norfolk man, Captain John Thompson, who became a Salem churchman. A relation, Captain Thomas Fiske, was an important and influential figure in Wenham, Massachusetts and in 1692, was foreman of the Salem witch trials jury. A member of a once-persecuted family had joined a faction of persecutors!

Insanity and horror in 'Witch City'

Arthur Miller's famous play *The Crucible* describes the horror of how Rebecca Nurse and other women were put on trial and hanged for witchcraft. Settlers at Salem feared dense forest close by where the native American Indians lived. Their terror fed wild imaginings and religious superstition and prejudice. It needed only a spark to set off one of the most insidious witch trials of history, and this came in the form of the hysterical accusations of a group of young girls.

Rebecca Nurse was 71 years old with a family of eight. Originally from Great Yarmouth in Norfolk, once settled in Salem Rebecca Towne married Francis Nurse. Rebecca was known to be a good, kind-hearted person. But her husband was in disputes over land including one with the Putnam family. The Putnams were later among Rebecca's accusers. Foremost among this group of accusers were the daughter and niece of Salem's minister,

The windswept Gallows Hill at Salem

Reverend Parris, with whom the Nurses also had some disagreements. Whether intentionally or subconsciously, it seems the minister had at least some influence on of the suspicion and hysteria that developed.

As with the witchcraft trials in England (Chapter 4), vicious lies were fabricated with claims that the mark of the devil was on Rebecca's body. Despite some support for Rebecca Nurse and her co-accused, the hysteria spread. Nurse was excommunicated, officially damned and abandoned to the devil! She and four others met their fate on the windswept Gallows Hill. In all, there were 20 executions, including Rebecca's sister Mary. Those like the Suffolk man John Proctor who opposed the trials, put their own lives in danger. Proctor was hanged for his bravery.

A number of the Norfolk people who had settled in Salem would have been involved with or at least touched by these trials, which shook the whole community and ultimately broke the power of the Puritans. The fanatical zeal had gone too far. Thomas Fiske and a number of others later confessed to having made a grave mistake. Even today, Salem is remembered as 'Witch City'. Tourists visit the church and the place where the accused were imprisoned. The town promotes an anti-prejudice message, but is not above reaping the commercial rewards of 'witch' merchandise; even taxis carry pictures of witches flying on broomsticks!

Mass exodus

Rebecca Towne and her Puritan family had left for America in the mid-1630s, when many Norfolk people were fleeing oppression. By 1637, Norfolk Puritans were leaving for the New World in droves aboard ships bearing names such as *John and Dorothy* and *The Rose*, to escape the persecution of Norwich's Anglican Bishop Wren.

Michael Metcalf, who owned a Norwich cloth factory, was among those who suffered from Wren's harsh measures. After losing his property Metcalf wrote, 'I was persecuted

1638, mass exodus from Hingham

in the land of my father's sepulchres, for not bowing at the name of Jesus, and observing other ceremonies in religion, forced upon me'... 'My enemies conspired against me to take away my life, and sometimes, to avoid their hands, my wife did hide me in the roof of the house, covering me over with straw.' Metcalf and his family escaped to Boston, where he became a schoolmaster.

In 1638 a mass exodus

from the town of Hingham in Norfolk, depleted it of a third of its residents. The leading rebel here was the Puritan Reverend Robert Peck, who had lost his post under Wren's oppression but had defied the bishop by conducting services in secret. Peck pulled down the chancel and altar rails, and under the threat of a summons before the London Court of High Commission, he decided that it was time to leave! He and his flock of about 200 people sailed to Boston and settled in New Hingham, already named by earlier settlers from the same village.

Many stayed on but, with others who were relieved to see the Puritans gain the upper hand in the English Civil War, Peck returned to his old Norfolk parish in 1646. Thomas Allen, a New England preacher who married the widow of Harvard College's founder, returned in 1651 to take charge of the Norwich parish, St. George Tombland.

From a Norfolk boy to Abraham Lincoln

The village of Hingham is famous not only for the fiery Peck and its mass exodus, but also for Abraham Lincoln's ancestor, Samuel Lincoln who was baptised in Hingham in 1622 and became an apprentice to Francis Lawes, a Norwich weaver. In 1637, he headed for New England with Lawes and his family, and made a home in New Hingham, Massachusetts.

Samuel's grandfather, a wealthy man who built a mansion in Swanton Morley, (now the Angel Pub), virtually disinherited his son Edward, choosing to leave most of his estate to his fourth wife and her family. Edward Lincoln struggled to make a living in Hingham and so Samuel had little to lose when he left England. Their misfortune could well have influenced the birth of one of the most important figures of the United States. Himself a fierce opponent of slavery, Abraham Lincoln led the northern states of America through the Civil War until his assassination in 1865, just before the final victory of the Union troops.

Many notable American rebels are descended from early Norfolk settlers. The Williams family is a prime example. Robert Williams, a Norwich cordwainer (leather-worker) and his wife Elizabeth were amongst those who arrived in the Massachusetts Bay Colony in 1637, having

The Angel Pub at Swanton Morley

sailed from Yarmouth. Their descendants include Louisa May Alcott, author of the novel *Little Women*, who modelled the unconventional character of Jo, a family rebel, on herself. General Joseph Warren, a radical leader and activist in the American Revolution, was another rebellious descendent of the Williams family. A war hero, he was killed in the battle at Bunker Hill in 1775. William Williams, who signed the Declaration of Independence, belonged to the same family.

The inspirational Thomas Paine

The man who inspired the American Revolution

Thomas Paine (1737-1809) was not only actively involved with the American Revolution, but also helped to inspire it. He was both a Norfolk rebel and one of the Founding Fathers of the United States of America – it was he who suggested the country's name.

The son of a Quaker, Paine was born in Thetford. A restless character, he left school early but never settled in any single job or profession. In 1774 while in London, he met Benjamin Franklin who proposed he emigrate to America. With Franklin's help, Paine left for Philadelphia where he found the freedom to express his radical ideas.

Sensing the dissatisfaction and rising tension in America, Thomas Paine published *Common Sense*, a treatise in support of American independence from Britain. The book sold extraordinarily well and encouraged many Americans to act on their desire for independence. Inspired at least in part by Paine's writing, George Washington went on to make the Declaration of Independence in 1776 (drafted by Thomas Jefferson), which remains America's most cherished symbol of liberty.

The War of Independence erupted the same year. Thomas Paine's American Crisis papers were very influential, including the rousing and oft-quoted words, 'These are the times that try men's souls'. Washington was so impressed by the first paper that he ensured it was read to his troops, to spur them on.

Paine was appointed to Congress but was forced to resign after he leaked secret information. He returned to England after a few years and soon turned his attention to the French Revolution, which he strongly defended in *Rights of Man* - writings that revealed both his social concerns and antimonarchy beliefs. The book was banned in royalist England, although he did find an American publisher. Paine was outlawed from his homeland, escaping to France just in time to avoid arrest for seditious libel.

Thomas Paine's support for the French Revolution did not protect him from imprisonment by Robespierre when he opposed the execution of Louis XVI. But putting his time to good use, in prison he wrote *The Age of Reason*, attacking organised religion as 'pious fraud'. It seems that he led a charmed life, for having avoided arrest in England, he now narrowly escaped execution in France. The chalk mark condemning him was accidentally drawn on the inside of his prison door while open, so when the time came to collect the prisoner for execution, his cell was passed by. Soon afterwards, Paine managed to obtain his release with the help of the U.S. Minister in France.

Despite his brush with death, Paine stayed in France for a few years and met Napoleon, who was so impressed that he suggested gold statues of Paine should be erected in his honour all over the world! Conversely, Paine did not take to Napoleon. A short while later, he returned to America at Thomas Jefferson's invitation, where despite all he had done for American independence, he was shunned and unpopular. The Age of Reason had turned the Americans against Paine who now saw him as an infidel. When he died in New York City, one newspaper gave him a cruel epitaph, 'He had lived long, did some good and much harm'. The Americans preached freedom and individuality, but Paine's independent spirit and beliefs went too far for them.

Thomas Paine was a brave and tragic rebel, widely regarded as a threat because of his nonconformity. Anti-monarchist, he was forced to stay away from England. Vocal in his disapproval of the political decision to execute the King, he was imprisoned by the French. And his religious criticism alienated him from the Americans he had supported and inspired.

An individual thinker ahead of his time, Thomas Paine nevertheless left an indelible mark. He had been known for his opposition to slavery, along with Amelia Opie, whom he knew through his close friendship with the radical intellectual William Godwin, partner of Mary Wollstonecraft. Harriet Martineau was another Norfolk rebel and writer who was a force in the antislavery movement. Like Thomas Paine, she took her ideals and convictions across the ocean to the United States.

The woman who challenged the American élite

Harriet Martineau (1802-1876) was born in Norwich into a family with Unitarian beliefs (Chapter 4). Life was not easy, ill health plaguing her childhood years. During Martineau's twenties, her father, brother and fiancé all died. Despite all the obstacles, she began to forge a successful writing career, driven by a strong will and intellectual curiosity.

Martineau was a known campaigner against slavery even before she travelled to the United States in 1834. In her first two years she immersed herself in her new society, meeting people from all walks of life, including Indians, slaves, prisoners and mental asylum patients, intellectuals and the rich elite. She chopped wood, stayed in log cabins and mansions, and was a guest at the White House! She was greatly disturbed by the treatment of slaves, as when she witnessed a woman and her children being sold at a slave market. Being entertained by the wealthy began to sit uncomfortably with her.

Martineau Memorial Hall, Norwich

An anti-slavery speech Harriet Martineau gave at a public meeting of abolitionists turned many Americans against her. Southerners threatened her with dire consequences if she ever dared to travel to the strongholds of slavery. People in the northern states reacted angrily to her concern for black women, who were discriminated against even in the 'free' north. Undeterred by the onslaught, she continued to express her beliefs and convictions in writing, noting that in its way America was a class-ridden society.

Martineau's *Society in America* was published on her return to England. Although appreciative of the generous welcome she received, she observed that American democratic ideals were not reflected in the way society was run. She developed a reputation for being controversial. Just as many Americans had turned against Thomas Paine for his atheistic leanings, so too many derided Harriet Martineau for daring to criticise their social structures and for supporting abolitionists, who were seen as a fanatical minority. In the tradition of a true rebel, Martineau was never afraid to make her feelings clear! During the last few years of her life, in spite of ill health, she continued to speak out for social justice and women's rights. She must have died content, for she lived to hear about the abolition of slavery after the American Civil War (1860-1865), and to know that she had played her part.

'Over-paid, over-sexed and over here'

With slavery outlawed, the Americans came closer to embracing their ideals of freedom and diversity. It was in this spirit that thousands of Americans came to Norfolk, and to many other English counties, in support of Britain's efforts to contain the Nazi threat in the Second World War. People had left Norfolk in droves, bound for the New World and liberation from repression; now many Americans were 'coming home' to defend the values and way of life of the Old World against a new oppressor.

Among the American soldiers and airmen who came to Norfolk were some famous names, such as Hollywood's Jimmy Stewart, who rejected an important MGM film contract in favour of fighting the war, much to the distress of his studio bosses! He is known to have visited Old Buckenham, Tibenham and Norwich while based in Norfolk. For a time he was at Ketteringham Hall, once the abode of Norfolk's Scarlet Pimpernel (Chapter 7) and later to become the home of Lotus Cars (Chapter 9).

The pioneering spirit was more in evidence than the puritanical one of early American settler days. These Americans tended to be loud and casual, with music to match, and with eccentric behaviour like smuggling in monkeys, snakes and parrots as pets! Many found Norfolk backward and dull and, not surprisingly, the relatively reserved Norfolk people did not always take to them. 'Over-paid, over-sexed and over-here' became a frequent refrain. Many women and young girls, however, found the US airmen attractive, with their racy big band

USAF men

music and fancy gifts. But the locals frowned on these relationships, regarding the women as rebels against the local way of life. Inevitably, tragic situations arose, as when a girl married an American GI only to discover he already had a wife back home. But there were successful marriages too and many of the 70,000 British girls who wed American servicemen were from East Anglia. This was the largest mass exodus of Norfolk people to America since the Puritan departure in the 1600s.

Romantic relationships apart, many liaisons and friendships were formed between Norfolk people and the Americans. Arthur Rush, who ran a pub in New Buckenham, had a good rapport with the Americans and a mind of his own. On one occasion, when an airman was drinking at his pub while officially confined to his station, the American military police came on a general inspection. Arthur hid the man in the coal cellar until they had gone, saving the GI a severe punishment.

The American airmen fought bravely and over 6,700 of those stationed in Norfolk and Suffolk lost their lives. But as in Vietnam and recently in Iraq, accidents occurred, including bombings into the Norfolk fields. Some of the men were trigger-happy. A scandal occurred when two GIs, George Smith and Leonard Wojtacha, stole ammunition for poaching on land at Honingham Hall near Norwich. The owner, Sir Eric Teichman, checking out the noise, was shot and both young men were subsequently executed for the crime.

There were also some strange events involving USAF airmen. In one story, several had refused to bomb Germany because they had family in the targeted area. They were linked to the mysterious destruction of aircraft and disappearance of bombers over the Channel and several men were executed. Locals claim that they were buried in the churchyard at Rougham. Though not home grown Norfolk rebels, these are men who lived and died there.

An on-going link

So, ironically, the Americans fought to save a country against which their ancestors had rebelled. In doing so, they had a lasting influence on that rejected land. Some of those who found themselves in Norfolk, must have been decendants of the many thousands who had originally fled for the New World. Norfolk rebels had played a major role in shaping early American society, whether as religious dissenters and adventurers, or as non-conformists and fighters for social justice.

A country that began as an escape from oppression itself became repressive. Then, the wheel turned again as they 'returned' to fight for freedom. Today, most Americans visiting Norfolk are there to re-discover just who their early rebel ancestors were.

The Norwich City library, The Forum, houses one of the best collections on America and its connections with Norfolk, and the University of East Anglia has a thriving American Studies department.

Norfolk's link with America, in so many ways brought about by Norfolk rebels, now involves a more peaceful and less rebellious exchange of interests and ideas.

The Norwich City Library: The Forum

Chapter Six

REBELATION OF THE SPIRIT

Rebelation Of The Spirit

ARTISTS WITH ATTITUDE

Many creative artists, including painters, sculptors, actors, dancers, musicians and writers who have rebelled in various ways have connections with Norfolk. Some have drawn on it for inspiration, while others have reacted against it. Many have challenged society as a whole.

Breaking the mould

Visual artists have often broken with tradition by employing new techniques. The Norwich Society of Artists, set up by John Crome in 1803 and known later as the Norwich School of Artists, developed a realistic style that was a radical move away from the idyllic art of painters like Thomas Gainsborough.

The work of J M W Turner, one of the great masters of landscape art and of watercolour, influenced the moody style of one of these Norwich artists, John Sell Cotman. Cotman also used light and dark, sometimes in blocks, in a way that resembled the cubist art of a century later. His early career flourished but later he fell from popularity.

Present day Norfolk artists who reject realism include sculptor and artist Pip Collyer, who creates abstract and simplified imagery, and painter Brian Lewis, whose strong colourful images of Norfolk

Knapton weathervane, designed by John Sell Cotman

contrast with the subtle traditional representations of the area.

From Pop Art to Science Fantasy

Some Norfolk-linked artists have influenced national and international art and culture. Colin Self, born in Norwich in 1941, studied at Norwich School of Art and then at the Slade in London. In the sixties he was a leading figure in the Pop Art movement. He searched for an art form to reflect a society that lived in the shadow of the Cold War and other social evils, while also imbuing that world with a sense of poetry. Although not a supporter of Pop Art's celebration of the material world, he viewed its illumination of everyday objects, fashion and other aspects of modern life as a working class reaction to elitist Fine Art. Colin Self saw himself as a cultural anarchist, and Pop Art as a major break with tradition.

While for Self this new style counteracted the negativity of the world by depicting its love and humanity, another rebel artist, Bruce Lacey, berated Pop Art for not addressing society's problems. Lacey was deeply concerned about the state of society, and influenced the culture of the sixties with an entirely different form of artistic rebellion.

Though a Norfolk resident for many years, Bruce Lacey was born in London in 1927 and lived there for the first part of his life. From early on his art and performance had shock-value. At college one performance was a dance with a female dummy that disintegrated. After studies at the Royal College of Art he formed the Alberts, an innovative anarchic comic jazz band that played bizarre instruments and satirised show business. His work is thought to have influenced the Bonzo Dog Doo Dah Band and the Beatles. Lacey also made props and created moving robotic figures, such as the auto-erotic hermaphrodite *The Womaniser*. He intended such creations to shake the observer into a sense of harsh reality. One image, of hands desperately trying to push through bamboo, reflected his anger about the state of society, third world poverty and war.

In the late sixties Lacey moved to a farmhouse near Wymondham, Norfolk, where he felt closer to the natural world. Here he created rituals based on alchemical and science fantasy themes, which he believed linked him to the earth goddess of energy and to the essence of artistic inspiration. He was a rebel with a difference who formed vivid expressions of his anger and crossed boundaries, linking the worlds of art, sculpture, performance and music in a way that created new perspectives.

An unorthodox clown and Buddhist

Another challenging performance artist who grew up in London and has now lived in Norfolk for many years is Cos Hardy. Like Bruce Lacey, he is strongly critical of society. Once a resident of the bohemian Argyle Street community in Norwich (Chapter), he refers to himself as an evolutionary humanist. He stands against exploitation and equally against enforcement of the law.

Cos Hardy, co-founder of The Foolhardy Folk

Hardy is co-founder of a co-operative clown troupe, the Foolhardy Folk, which seeks to highlight human stupidity. Social and political criticism underlies the clowning. They have explored themes such as a post-nuclear world and the problem of red tape. In 2004 the BBC3 programme *Not Under My Roof* showed how Hardy had taken a completely divergent path from his Greek Orthodox father, who had hoped his son would settle down as a Christian with a conventional job. Spending time together while filming the programme healed the rift of misunderstanding between them.

Hardy's sights are set on another television programme based on a visit to the Buddha tree at Sarnath in India with his friend Shanton Seth. Brother of the novelist Vikram Seth, Shanton is a Gandhian who has made a big impact on the Norwich peace movement and has since been employed by the United Nations to help stop the practice of cannibalism in remote areas of the world. A Buddhist, Hardy believes that humanity is about to destroy the planet, and is seeking to create a more sharing, peaceful world.

Cos Hardy's clown troupe is one of a number of alternative performance groups in Norfolk that defy traditional methods and thinking. The Norfolk and Norwich Festival has plans for a Street Festival for similar groups, such as the Theatre of Adventure in Norwich, which seek to transform every day situations into a musical.

From folk to punk

Beth Orton is a musician who started off in alternative theatre. Born in Norwich, where she lived until her teens when the family moved to London, she created an unorthodox sound which fuses acoustic folk with modern electronic rhythms. The successful Norwich-based band Cord, which has been compared to Radiohead, also strives for a new and innovative sound.

Many bands are challenging in their appearance, sound or lyrics. A well-known rebellious band from the region that falls into this category is the heavy 'Glam-Rock' act, The Darkness. Its members hail from Yarmouth's old rival town of Lowestoft, just over the Suffolk border, but they also have links with Norfolk. The flamboyant lead singer is Justin Hawkins, whose image is now in Madame Tussaud's. He and his brother Dan decided to form a band when it became clear that Justin had talent – displayed by his impressively exuberant form of karaoke in their aunt's Norfolk pub! The band's lyrics are intended to instil fear or to shock. Drawing on their East Anglian roots, one song depicts the terrifying Black Shuck, a dog that is believed to have haunted lonely corners of Norfolk and other eastern counties for hundreds of years.   Those unfortunate enough to catch his single eye die soon afterwards, or someone they know suffers that fate. A legend brought to life by smugglers, Black Shuck features in Chapter 8.

Cley-next-the-Sea, a north Norfolk coastal village with a long tradition of smuggling, is also linked with the successful singer-songwriter James Blunt.   His family has owned Cley windmill for many years, his father was brought up there and James himself spent time at the mill. Blunt's father, like his father before him, was in the military, and James was expected to follow the family tradition. He did join up and served in the

Justin Hawkins, The Darkness

army for four years, but his heart was set on music. Putting disappointment aside, his family supported him as he followed the dream that led to great success, including a Number One hit in the States in 2006.

Pirates, ahoy!

A far cry from the Harrow-educated James Blunt, a number of Punk bands have sprung up out of Norfolk, including one called Rebelation, which somehow speaks for itself! Kunk, a rhythm and blues cum punk band from Norwich, gained publicity after disk jockey John Peel played Public Image Ltd on the radio. Peel, who died in 2004, was well known for promoting new, provocative or innovative sounds.

In the sixties John Peel was involved with the offshore 'pirate' radio station, Radio Caroline, which he called East Anglian radio's jewel in the crown until it was closed down by the government in 1967.   Keith Skues, later presenter of BBC Radio's late night programme in the Eastern Counties, was once a pirate broadcaster for Radio Caroline. As pirate stations like Caroline were located off the east coast, a number of Norfolk people became involved, including Andy Archer who also worked for BBC Radio Norfolk. A native of Terrington St. Clement, Norfolk, Archer had a spell with the RAF before joining Radio Caroline and re-joining when it re-opened in the seventies as an illegal operation. He was fined twice under the Marine Offences Act, in the seventies and again in the eighties.

Exposing and promoting the good ol' boys

While real-life DJs have upset the system by working on pirate radio stations, one fictional DJ has also caused a stir with Norfolk residents. Steve Coogan's creation of Norwich DJ Alan Partridge in *I'm Alan Partridge*, has been accused of ridiculing Norfolk people by portraying them as country bumpkins. Comedy's pastiche and exaggeration give it the cloak of rebellion too. Steve Coogan, who has urged television bosses to go back to basics instead of following fashion, clearly sympathises with the Partridge character. Rebellion can come in yet another form - the struggle against change! A big advocate of the old Norfolk ways and dialect is the home-grown Norfolk writer, presenter and entertainer, Keith Skipper. In his fight against the flow of so-called 'progress', Skipper has written books about the Norfolk dialect and people. He stands up for the uniqueness of the county at a time when many local characteristics are being muted or obliterated. Having worked at Norfolk Radio, Skipper now writes for the *Eastern Daily Press* and tours the county with popular comedy sketches about the Norfolk 'ol' boys'!

Stephen Fry, rebellious by nature

A rebel bound for great success

Stephen Fry is a successful and multi-talented writer, comedian and actor who is a Norfolk man and champions 5 the Canaries (Norwich City Football Club). Although he was born in London, he was brought up in Booton, the birthplace of the Norfolk Jacobite Christopher Layer, near Reepham. Rebellious by nature, Fry revels in practical jokes, sometimes on an epic scale – so much so that as a youngster he was expelled from two schools. While studying at Cambridge University, he met Hugh Laurie and Emma Thompson, and focused his energy and talent positively through entertainment and writing. His sharp wit was reflected in works that ridiculed the English buffoon, as Blackadder did. Open in his homosexuality and concerned to connect with the truth of his inner self, his characterisation of Oscar Wilde in the film Wilde, released in 1997, was outstanding. Whereas Oscar Wilde had the misfortune of living in an era of cruel intolerance, Fry has the freedom be himself without the crippling hindrance of a bigoted society, and to delight people with his wit and intelligence.

An actor with strong convictions

Yet another Norfolk-based actor with a rebellious streak is Martin Shaw, who played Doyle in the television series *The Professionals* and recently the title role in *Judge John Deed*. He also starred as a rebel chief constable at odds with the Home Office in *The Chief*, which was filmed in Norwich. He and his wife Vicky live in a converted Quaker Meeting House that once belonged to an ancestor of Abraham Lincoln. Even as a child, Shaw held strongly individual views, and hated school.

A vegetarian, Shaw has produced a cookbook and supports a range of charities and causes for the humane treatment of animals. He was involved with the campaign to save a boar,

Hillside Animal Sanctuary

nicknamed McQueen, which had made a 'great escape' from a slaughterhouse. With his wife, Shaw once broke into a Norfolk duck farm to rescue two sick birds from what they believed to be a 'concentration camp' for ducks. The angry farmer initially mistook them for animal rights activists, saying that the ducks were not worth saving. But the Shaws nursed them back to health, naming them Eric and Ernie after the comedians, and later donating them to Hillside Animal Sanctuary, in Frettenham, Norfolk.

Rejecting tradition

Arnold Wesker's well-known play *I'm talking about Jerusalem*, written in 1960, is set in rural Norfolk and based on the experience of his sister and her husband. Wesker also lived in Norfolk for a time, giving him an understanding of its people and culture. As one of the main instigators of 'Kitchen Sink' drama, he was instrumental in breaking the mould of British playwriting, which had up until that time been mainly based on middle and upper class society. He pushed for theatre to be more accessible to everybody. A social rebel, Wesker joined the Young Communist League in his early years. In 1961 he served a month in prison for being part of the Committee of 100 and their disruptive action in Trafalgar Square.

Wesker was born into a Jewish family in London in 1932. Later, he worked in Norwich as a kitchen porter at the Bell Hotel, of Hell Fire Club infamy! Here he met his future wife Doreen. He based one of his most famous plays, Roots, on her Norfolk family writing of the need to free oneself from the chains of convention and to find ones own ideas and form of communication. His plays express a belief in personal freedom as well as a social concern.

Ian McEwan, author of *Atonement* and the Booker Prize winning *Amsterdam*, is another mouldbreaker with Norfolk links. He is one of a number of successful authors who have passed through the highly regarded creative writing course at the University of East Anglia. From the start his UEA tutors were delighted with his dark writings, often involving taboo topics. At odds with his domineering father, an army man who tyrannised his mother, as a young man McEwan wrote on shocking subjects such as incest or infanticide. Like Arnold Wesker, he rebelled against a tradition of writers involved with middle and upper class values and became known for his hard-hitting social commentary.

Less challenging but equally thought-provoking in his writings is Kazuo Ishiguro, another ex-UEA creative writing student. Originally from Nagasaki, Japan, his novels question the status quo in a subtle way, exposing the social situations that can trap people, as in the Booker Prize winning *Remains of the Day*. The celebrated novelist Rose Tremain, who taught UEA's course, looks at how personal feelings can lead to entrapment. Her books, such as *Restoration* which was set in seventeenth century Norfolk and London (later made into a film), deal with outsiders led by love and passion.

The late writer Lorna Sage, whose autobiography *Bad Blood* won the Whitbread Biography award in 2001, was

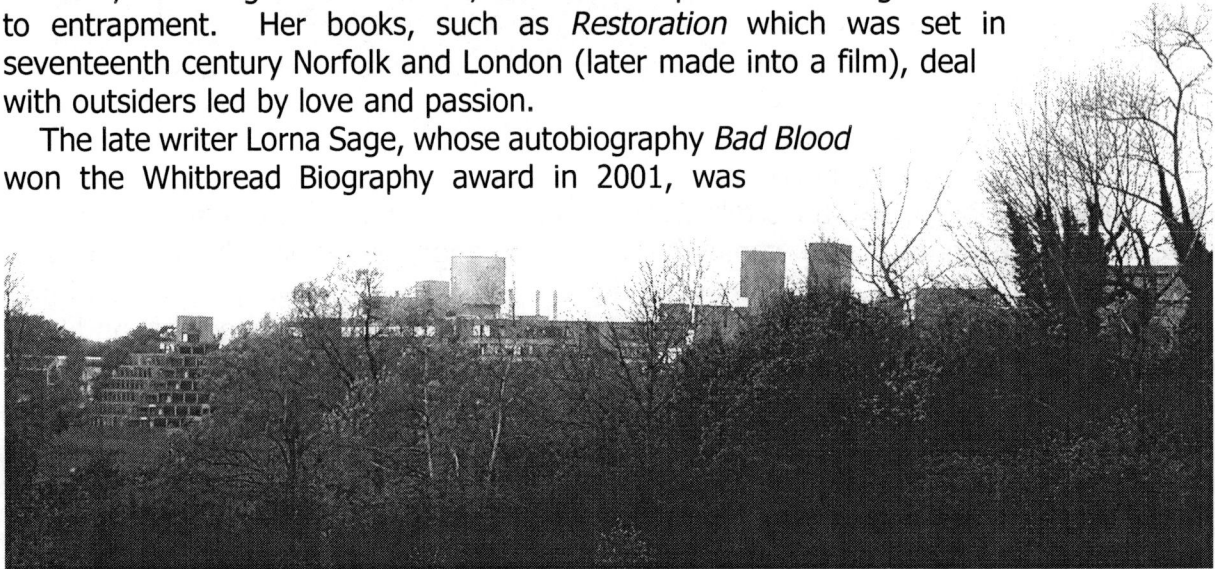

Many controversial writers have studied at UEA

Professor of Literature at UEA. In *Bad Blood* she describes her upbringing on the Welsh border, pregnancy at age sixteen and local scandal. In the face of disapproval Sage had the child and married the father, escaping to a semi-bohemian life and success at university. Another book by Sage (*Angela Carter*) was about her close friend, the writer Angela Carter whose challenging blend of fantasy and hard-hitting erotic, sometimes savage themes dealing with personal initiation, intrigued Sage. This is perhaps not surprising, as Sage herself had managed to transform despair, hurt and anger into joy and personal victory. She refused to be restricted by society's expectations.

A partisan and a hostage

Frederick Forsyth, author of the best-selling thriller *The Day of the Jackal*, began his writing career in Norfolk while a journalist on the *Eastern Daily Press*. After a BBC posting in Africa, he free lanced in Biafra, where he supported the Biafran people in the Nigerian civil war of the 1960's, and became a partisan. His subsequent books reflect his observation of dishonesty and corruption while in the West African state. For instance, *The Dogs of War* describes the greed and opportunism behind a plan to overthrow an African government. He is an author who challenges governments and corruption, and exposes what he sees as the flaws in society.

Anthony Grey, a writer who was brought up in Norwich and lives there today, has explored the way in which both personal relationships and social ideals can cause people to find themselves at odds with larger social forces. A number of his epic novels, such as *Saigon* and *Peking* deal with rebellion on a massive scale. In *Saigon*, he talks about the repression inherent in colonialism giving rise to 'the hatred of a million coolies'.

Grey's novels portray people who stand up for their ideals in the face of oppression, social disapproval and cruelty. He was himself just such an outsider when in 1967 at the time of Mao's Cultural Revolution, he was taken hostage while working as a journalist for Reuters in Peking. Guilty only of being British, he was locked up in one room of his house for two years and used as a bargaining tool. He suffered death threats and many kinds of psychological torture. He was eventually released, and the trauma he experienced subsequently spurred on both his writing and the

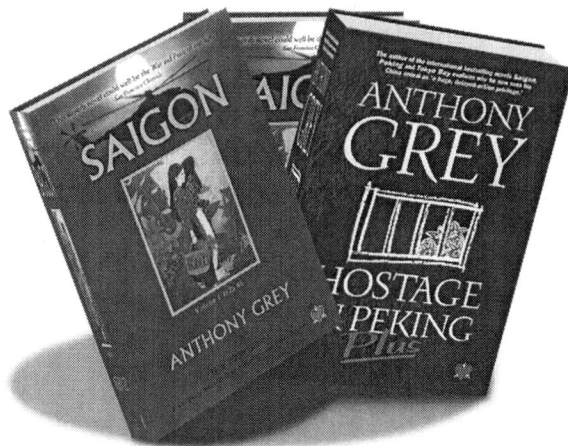

Anthony Grey's books: thought provoking

development of unorthodox social and spiritual views that challenge accepted beliefs and ideas.

Accused of blasphemy

One of today's most famous authors, Philip Pullman was born in Norwich in 1946. He has been accused of blasphemy, for his writings reflect views diametrically opposed to his Christian upbringing. Pullman's grandfather was Rector of Drayton and later became Norwich Prison's chaplain, so as a boy he gained an intimate understanding of the religion he was later to repudiate. He detests in particular the more dogmatic religious sects, and in an *Eastern Daily Press* interview he referred to the Pilgrim Fathers as obnoxious! He believes they are at the root of much presentday American Christian thinking, such as accepting the biblical creation story as literal truth. His *Dark Materials* trilogy involves a repressive god who wants Lyra, the heroine, to be killed in order to stop her from being tempted by the knowledge that will enable her to flourish. Through the medium of fantasy fiction, he criticises the nullifying rigidity of organised religion, believing that the human mind should always be open and enquiring.

Like Wesker's Beatie in *Roots* who finally realises the enlivening effect of asking questions, Philip Pullman rejects any form of blind acquiescence. For both Wesker and Pullman, self-empowerment is central to their thinking. Norfolk writers like Lorna Sage, a victim of small-town prejudice, and Anthony Grey, a long-term hostage, empowered themselves by overcoming adversity with creativity and hard work.

A hotbed of creative rebellion!

Norfolk's creative rebels have made their mark not just on Norfolk, but on the wider world. Many broke away from a traditional culture they viewed as elitist. Arnold Wesker's 'Kitchen Sink' drama, Ian McEwan's disturbing social observations and Bruce Lacey's artistic expression of society's ills, all reveal bold moves away from the beaten track of accepted thinking. Others, like Philip Pullman, have challenged the essence of traditional belief and unquestioning acceptance. Whether through the visual arts, music, acting or language, they have broadened the perspectives of millions of people, opening up whole new areas of thinking and creative expression.

Chapter Seven

REFUGEES AND RENEGADES

Refugees And Renegades

LIFE ON THE OUTSIDE

Some people find themselves in the rebel camp simply by being different. Whether they are foreigners with their cultures, communities experimenting with a new way of living, or individuals at odds with conventional expectations, they are often viewed as society's 'black sheep'. As colourful misfits and outsiders they attract both fascination and antagonism.

From old ways...

History gives us many examples of people rebuffed purely for following tradition. The Kitty Witches of Great Yarmouth donned male garments and smeared their faces with blood, before running through the narrowest street in town to beg money for drinks. This old ritual was considered superstitious and anti-Christian and was stamped out in the nineteenth century. In Victorian society the followers of folk customs were outsiders, and considered uncivilised.

Echoes in a narrow Yarmouth street

...to new ways

Even today, gypsies remain the butt of such prejudice against old ways. And those who experiment with new forms of living still find themselves marginalised.

One such controversial alternative community made its home in central Norwich. It thrived for a few years living in caravans and trailers, as well as the houses of Argyle Street. 'Hippies', 'travellers' and others looking for an alternative way of life were welcomed there. Some had dropped out of society and others were involved with bands, bookshops, alternative food shops and spiritual activities such as tai chi. They resented interference from the 'outer' community, preferring to sort out problems between themselves rather than alert the police. Some people, including members of Norwich City Council, viewed them as disreputable troublemakers. Others, particularly the elderly, welcomed them for the help they gave to those in need. One Argyle Street resident was elected to the Council on an Anarchist ticket, reflecting popular support. Rather than take up his seat, he worked within the community, earning notoriety for his arrest for daubing graffiti on the front of City Hall! Later he became a Labour Councillor but, finding it too restrictive, soon left.

Community wiped out

In 1982, the Council decided to rid Norwich of the Argyle Street community and had the buildings demolished to make way for a new development. Protests were to no avail and families were re-housed. Shortly before demolition the vacated properties were occupied by a strange mélange of unorthodox characters. Having lost hope, the remaining inhabitants set about gutting the houses. On the last night they held a wild party and started a number of fires. They barricaded the end of the road so that neither the police nor the fire brigade could enter. In the morning they all left in an exodus travelling to Thetford to join the Peace Convoy there.

Argyle Street, 1982

Clashes with police

The Peace Convoy was a group of travellers that moved around the country participating in festivals and peace campaigns along the way. The convoy began in the eighties, and a few still travel the country today. They visited Norwich at the time of a Green Fair at the university, illegally settling there after the fair but soon forced to move on. Even Margaret Thatcher, Prime Minister at that time expressed her disapproval and determination to curb their activities. At Stonehenge in the mid eighties the Peace Convoy, including some Norfolk people, was involved in clashes with riot police. A number of protestors were wounded, and it was some of these young people from Norfolk who approached the police with an offer to help everyone leave the area in an orderly way if they could be left alone to sort it out. The police let people go without retribution on condition that they departed by an agreed route.

The Romany way

Gypsies are travellers who have long had problems finding sites in which they can legally set up camp and are still today regarded as outsiders. Traditionally a travelling community, although some have now settled, the gypsies are mainly Romanies who make up a large ethnic group in Norfolk. They came originally from India about a thousand years ago, beginning to settle in Norfolk in the early sixteenth century. From the start they were persecuted and treated as scapegoats because of their foreign ways and unfamiliar religion and customs. During the sixteenth and seventeenth centuries many were deported and a number were hanged, notably thirteen were hanged together in Suffolk.

Most gypsies still leading a partially nomadic existence today have abandoned their traditional horse-drawn caravans for motorised trailers, though they maintain many of their beliefs and ways. John Leveridge is an exception to this rule; he travels around Norfolk in a traditional horse-drawn wagon with his family, though he also has a house outside Norwich and a car. However, as much as he can he follows the old Romany way of his forebears, who were also Norfolk-based gypsies, travelling in the summer and visiting fairs. Another gypsy still in touch with the old ways is known as Patrick, whose faith enables him to walk through fire. His friends describe him as 'simple but profound'.

A heart in foreign lands

George Henry Borrow (1803-1881) was a Norfolk man who became fascinated by gypsies. Encouraged in his early years by the Norwich scholar, William Taylor, Borrow became a successful writer. Educated in Norwich and then in Edinburgh, he travelled widely and became closely acquainted with European gypsies. Against the grain of the prevailing antagonism towards gypsies, Borrow upheld their culture and customs in his writings, as in his books *Lavengro* and *Romany Rye*.

Borrow clearly did not hold the Norwich citizens in such high regard. In his translation of Von Klinger's *Faustus, his Life, Death and Descent into Hell*, he wrote of people 'with such ugly figures and flat features that the devil owned he had never seen them equalled, except by the inhabitants of an English town, called Norwich, when dressed in their Sunday best.' Not surprisingly, libraries threw his publication onto the flames! Borrow eventually came to

George Henry Borrow

84

appreciate his own land, but for years he was scathing about the English and considered an outsider by virtue of his views and affiliations to other cultures.

Tragedy at Bleak House

In contrast, an equally independent Norfolk man, Tony Martin, developed an intense dislike of gypsies. Born in 1944 in Wisbech, just over the border in Cambridgeshire, he travelled to various countries, before, at age thirty-five, he settled in the

Tony Martin's remote fenland

remote Norfolk fen-land at Bleak House. He lived a virtually hermit-like existence, alone with his pet rottweilers in the isolated, dilapidated house filled with clutter and covered in foliage. Those who knew him agreed he was an eccentric and one friend referred to him as 'his own man'. Martin was burgled on more than one occasion and took to sleeping at night with his boots on and a gun by his side. In an incident which made Martin the focus of national publicity, he shot a 16-year old burglar who subsequently died; he happened to be a gypsy. This was a tragedy involving two completely different types of 'outsiders'. Martin eventually won an appeal against the charge of murder, and was released after some three years in prison. Today he is an advocate for people living in fear, as he did, and although he regrets what happened, he expresses strong opinions against both burglars and gypsies.

Tony Martin is not the only voice on what is a deep and complex issue. For years in this remote fenland around Bleak House, there has been mutual resentment between gypsies and some of the local residents. While a few of the gypsies have committed burglary and other minor crimes, many feel they are victims of intolerance. Even in the Norwich area, John Leveridge, who is guilty only of following his family's traditional culture, has repeatedly suffered abuse.

A haven for refugees

Across Europe for centuries gypsies have attracted prejudice because of their way of life which is at odds with conventional communities. Adolf Hitler inflamed public prejudice against gypsies. At least a million were put to death in concentration camps where many others from minority ethnic groups, most notably six million Jews, also died.

In contrast, (Chapter 4) the Norwich Jewish community thrives today. In 2004 they helped to mount Kinder Transport, an exhibition at Norwich Cathedral about the lifesaving transportation of Jewish children from Nazi Germany and other Nazi controlled areas to England. Some of these children later became the Norwich Jews. One man, who as a child had been transported from German occupied Czechoslovakia to Norfolk, remembered how the children were taken from one door to another until someone agreed to take them in. Unable to speak English and forced to leave their parents behind, they felt homesick and uprooted. In many cases they never saw their parents again.

Although Norwich is home to fewer foreigners than many other British cities, it has provided a haven for refugees. In the 1970s and 1980s a number of these were Chileans, fleeing Pinochet's cruel regime. Some of them became involved in a group set up to support those suffering from oppression in South and Central America. They also created a supportive link between Norwich and the Nicaraguan town of El Viejo. Even Norwich's famous football club, the Canaries, became involved inviting a group of youngsters from El Viejo to come and play football in the Canary Cup youth tournament.

A black community from the Communist Party of South Africa used to live in Norwich's Argyle Street. A spiritual man known as Black Gerry lived there too. A fan of H.G.Wells, he was considered a wise man and became known as the Argyle Street guru.

'The Prostitutes' Padre'

Harold Francis Davidson (1875-1937) was a totally different kind of unconventional spiritual guide – a renegade vicar who ended up working in a circus! Through time, conflicting attitudes to sexuality has created rebels in the religious sphere. Harold Davidson, the Vicar of the north Norfolk village of Stiffkey and known as 'the Prostitute's Padre' is a colourful example. A graduate of Oxford University, he held prestigious jobs at Holy Trinity, Windsor, and St. Martins-in-the- Fields, in London's Trafalgar Square.

Later, when rector at Stiffkey, he married and had a family. The rector began to spend an increasing amount of time away from home. His marriage came under pressure when it became apparent that he was spending his time helping attractive young prostitutes in London, even

The rector of Stiffkey, fatally mauled by Freddie the Lion

bringing some of these 'saved fallen women' back to Stiffkey to be introduced to the family. The Bishop of Norwich informed an enraged Church hierarchy of Davidson's so-called immorality and he was banned from preaching in church. Although the locals joked about him, many found him charismatic and listened to his sermons in the open air.

The rector was eventually defrocked. He had always been eccentric, once riding his bicycle straight into the church and up the aisle to the pulpit, so a second 'career' in show business is perhaps not so farfetched! In fairs and circuses, he stood on a barrel to proclaim his innocence and to read the Bible. He went on hunger strike in his barrel, lay on a bed of nails wearing a loincloth, and staged an act where Satan's pitchfork prodded him while he was being cooked in an oven! Eventually, he was fatally mauled by Freddie the lion during his *Daniel in the Lion's Den* act. The flamboyant film director Ken Russell immortalised Harold Davidson in the *Lion's Mouth*, a short film about this bizarre rebel vicar!

Bigamy and wives for sale

Until the late nineteenth century it was difficult for anyone to change the rules of conventional married life. It was impossible for the poor to get divorced because of the prohibitive expense of it, so people unable to cope with unhappy marriages were forced to break the law. Desertion of a marital partner was illegal, although it happened, as did bigamy.

John Mason of Thetford was sentenced to 12 years in penal servitude in Australia for having two wives. John Green of King's Lynn sold his wife in the market place for no more than a barrel of beer, a price he was content to take given his addiction to alcohol.

As the public reaction to Mary Wollstonecraft showed (Chapter 2), women who departed from their 'allotted place' in society were frowned upon. One woman who successfully made her mark in this man's world was Alicia Meynell from Norwich. She rode her horse at the York races in the early 1800s at a time when being a jockey was a strict male preserve, beating the celebrated jockey Frank Buckle, much to his embarrassment!

The Norfolk Scarlet Pimpernel

Another woman who followed her own calling was the actress Charlotte Atkyns, otherwise known as the Norfolk Scarlet Pimpernel. Her mission began soon after meeting and befriending Marie Antoinette at Versailles when Charlotte and her wealthy husband, Robert Atkyns of Ketteringham Hall, were travelling the continent. Distraught at the news that Marie Antoinette had been imprisoned under sentence of death, she disguised herself as a soldier as part of a plan to help her friend to escape. As history has told, she failed in her attempt and Marie Antoinette was executed.

After her husband's death Charlotte Atkyns devoted an enormous amount of time and money on ambitious plots to rescue the Dauphin and to help him escape France. She ended her days in poverty and was buried in an unmarked grave in Paris in 1836. Her plight ignited some compassion and in 1907 a plaque in her memory was placed in Ketteringham Church.

'A nurse who tried to do her duty'

Edith Cavell (1865-1915) was born in Swardeston, a village near Norwich. Cavell, who successfully helped many people to escape from the oppressive German occupation in Belgium, was regarded as a heroine in Britain, but as a renegade by the German forces. She went to work as a nurse for the Red Cross in Brussels at the beginning of the First World War, turning her efforts to helping fugitives and escapees leave the country. In doing so she was putting her own life in danger because from the Germans' point of view she was abusing the protection they allowed Red Cross workers. After about a year she was caught and under interrogation she confessed. Her admittance came partly from her belief that she should never tell a lie. She was sentenced to death. It appears that at the point of her execution, the selflessness of her actions inspired rebellion. It was reported that one soldier in the firing squad refused to fire and so was shot for disobedience. Edith Cavell was loved by many and the Allies proclaimed her a martyr, though she saw herself only as 'a nurse who tried to do her duty.'

Edith Cavell: a brave woman

Pushing the boundaries

People who commit themselves to acts of compassion, keeping old traditions alive or seeking an alternative way of life are often seen as a threat to social stability. But in following their consciences or introducing new ways and ideas, these social rebels also help to create a freer and ultimately more tolerant world. Some have paved the way for more personal freedom, such as women's equality or the right to divorce. Others have challenged Norfolk folk to respect all the ways in which people might wish to 'du different'!

The Norwich of today reflects this respect for difference in its ethnic restaurants, music of all types and cultures, alternative food and bookshops, and special interest groups engaged in everything from martial arts to shamanic healing. 'Outsiders' of every kind have brought colour and diversity to the rich tapestry of life in Norfolk.

Norwich of today - social diversity in the busy marketplace

Chapter Eight

PIRATES, CONTRABAND AND BURNING PARSONS

Pirates, Contraband and Burning Parsons

THE ROGUES OF NORFOLK'S PAST

Following a different way of life, off society's beaten track, sometimes means taking a darker, lawless path. To the modern mind, rogues of years-gone-by conjure romantic images of highwaymen demanding 'Stand and deliver!' or of Johnny Depp's exotic pirate in the film *Pirates of the Caribbean*, and we are drawn to root for the brigand, however cruel. But reality was and is generally a lot grubbier, terrifying for the victims and ultimately gruesome for the perpetrators.

A spirited highwayman

Right up until the common land enclosures and the arrival of the railways in the nineteenth century, travelling from one town to another could be perilous. Highwaymen often lurked in wild, remote spots, where it was easy to disappear after their encounters. Horses were easy to spook and a pistol was enough to intimidate. Many highwaymen operated in Norfolk. Joseph Beeton was active until 1782, when he stopped a post boy who was travelling on horseback between King's Lynn and Wisbech and forced him to hand over the mailbags. Beeton was caught after this incident and was gaoled at King's Lynn. He escaped, but was caught again and sentenced to death. An independent rule-breaker to the last, he jumped as soon as the rope was round his neck, to ensure that it was he, not the hangman, who controlled this final act. His body was put into a gibbet close to the point at which he had stolen the mailbags, as a warning to other potential robbers or highwaymen. The dead were often left in the dangling gibbets until their flesh had rotted away and their crumbling bones fell out through the bars.

An artful dodger pirate

Another shady character who suffered the same grisly fate was the Norfolk pirate William Payne (1738-1781). As captain of the *Cerf-Volant*, he would seize other boats and steal what he wanted. He managed to avoid capture until finally his boat was forced to land near Southwold. A number of his men were caught, but Payne, an artful dodger, managed to slip away. When the authorities caught up with him in a nearby inn, they found him smoking in a relaxed manner. Payne audaciously produced Letters of Marque to 'prove' his connection to the French Admiralty and claimed to be an American citizen, no doubt with the appropriate accent! But his powers of deception could not save him; he was soon recognised as having come from Northrepps in Norfolk. William Payne was hanged and for many years his remains hung in a gibbet in Great Yarmouth to warn people of the consequences of piracy. This spot came to be called Payne's Hill. The year before Payne's capture, the American pirate, Captain Daniel Fall of the *Fearnought*, proved to be an unrelenting menace for other vessels until a Yarmouth revenue cutter successfully attacked him; later, he was chased away by a ship under Horatio Nelson's command.

The power of the Norfolk pirates

Norfolk's home-grown pirates, or 'privateers' as they were sometimes called, were recorded as being active around the Norfolk coast in the Middle Ages, and no doubt had been for centuries before that. In the fourteenth century they had virtual control of Cley on the North Norfolk coast, and there were reports of their activities at nearby Morston in the 1500s. By the eighteenth century, some of them were even given Letters of Marque to allow them to attack enemy vessels with impunity! The Great Yarmouth cutters were given free reign to seize French ships, and French privateers attacked the British during the 1741-48 war with France. So pirates who followed these rules gained the official stamp of approval. Smugglers also thrived at times of war, with each enemy camp using them to serve their own ends. Moreover, when soldiers were away there was less likelihood of resistance and the smugglers, many of whom were pirates, had free rein.

Norfolk smugglers in action

Over the centuries, the remoteness and expanse of the North Norfolk coast as made it a haven for smugglers. Daniel Defoe, author of the classic novel *Robinson Crusoe* said that 'the art of smuggling was so much in practice' in Morston. Fights between smugglers and law

The Morston mudflats

enforcers frequently ended with fatalities. The smugglers usually found those who were paid to stop them fairly easy to deal with – sometimes by tying to a tree! But the smugglers were more nervous of the dragoons, who confronted them in organised groups and were well armed. A typical incident occurred in the Morston area in 1817 when one group of smugglers plied the dragoons with copious quantities of alcohol in Cley's Swan Inn, while others went with their carts to wait for the boats carrying the contraband.

The Norfolk smugglers were well practised in the art of trickery, duping those they thought were on their trail. They also liked to frighten people whom they thought would interfere or cause trouble. The smugglers would tie a lantern to a large black ram or dog, and send it through the streets on dark nights. Believing it to be the dreaded ghostly curse of death, known as the hound Black Shuck, the terrorised people would stay indoors.

Cley waterways

Smugglers imprisoned

After the *1736 Smugglers Act*, smugglers faced execution if caught and many who refused to give themselves up became outlaws. Rewards were offered for their capture and a number were put to death. Many of the prisoners who languished in the appalling conditions of Norwich Castle were smugglers and often died there. Escape seemed a better way, and some succeeded. In 1733 the five Kimberley smugglers made their get-away with outside help after attacking the gaoler and taking away the keys, throwing them on a dunghill as they rode off into the countryside! Of those who managed to escape, some went to sea, a number of them never returning to England.

A groundswell of support!

Smugglers found allegiances in the most unlikely places. Sometimes officers expelled from the Preventive service joined the smugglers! And many local people were themselves involved in smuggling, or at least in league with them, attracted by the ability to buy cheap tobacco or gin.

The extent of the smugglers' support was revealed by several happenings. After a sea chase in 1822, in which a boat called the *Ranger* pursued a smuggling boat for 12 hours, some of the smugglers were captured and thrown into Yarmouth gaol. The following day when being led back to the *Ranger* for transfer elsewhere, a crowd threw stones at the officers. Shortly afterwards, residents in nearby Happisburgh were accused of not responding to the *Ranger's* distress signals when it ran aground. The crew perished, and although the inhabitants of Happisburgh denied hearing anything, they did not express regret– perhaps due to the smuggling gang that operated in their midst, from the Manor House at Happisburgh. Villagers of Hungry Hill, Northrepps, were paid for their assistance to the smugglers. By the 1880s armed gangs of smugglers were in virtual control of parts of the North Norfolk coast.

Windmill operators along the coast would use the sails of the mills to give

Happisburgh Manor House

Windmill sails were used to give signals to smugglers

signals to the smugglers, and allowed storage of smuggled goods. Barges helped with transport. Innkeepers were involved too, the spirits that they served often being smugglers' booty. A story goes that at the Cherry Tree Inn at Plumstead, excise officers were distracted with food and alcohol while smuggled barrels were swiftly removed, and were nowhere to be found by the time the officers were ready to search!

Smugglers often also had 'respectable' jobs. Farmers, for example, engaged in the smuggling of wool. Mark Butcher (1734-1809), a farmer from Earsham, was believed to have amassed a lot of money from smuggling liquor. He created a large, ornate tomb for himself a number of years before he died and many people thought he stored contraband in it!

Shady men of the cloth

Men of the cloth were particularly incongruous bedfellows for smugglers. But there were churchmen in Norfolk who operated in the same vein as the infamous Dr. Christopher Syn from Dymchurch on the desolate Romney Marsh. A Kentish vicar by day, he became known as the 'Scarecrow' by night. In the early twentieth century the Reverend George Phillips of Gorleston, near Yarmouth, claimed that a rector had once built some sizeable cellars underneath the vicarage to store smuggled goods. Moreover, at the shady rector's instigation, a subterranean passage had been dug between the cellars and a landing area for boats. In 1789, when a new arrival in the area asked if there was no one – such as a minister – to deal with the smugglers, someone pointed to the vicar, who at that moment was holding up a lantern for a group of smugglers! Yet another rector allowed smugglers to make use of his barn, strategically situated close to Hickling Broad, which was linked to some of their most used waterways.

Remote, wild and dangerous

The Broads were a favourite haunt for the smugglers, who hid their contraband in the reeds, and who would weave through the waterways deep into the countryside. Lonely and remote, the area provided protection for smugglers and was home to other dubious characters. In the nineteenth century a group of wild herring shovellers, known as the Roaring Boys, twentieth century the Reverend George Phillips lived at Hickling. One of the more law-abiding members of the clergy was unlucky enough to get on to the wrong side of the Roaring Boys and was burned on a bonfire by the lawless, angry gang. The Roaring Boys were resentful of the power and wealth of the clergy, which was in sharp contrast to the poverty of the local people, and of their efforts to enforce law and order. As described in Chapter 1, the starving poor of the countryside resorted to food riots , and poaching was commonplace.

Until the mid-nineteenth century, the remoter parts of Norfolk had very little outside interference, making them ripe for smuggling and other illicit activities. Villages like Briston and Edgefield, known for the magical arts such as healing and tarot reading, were notoriously

The Norfolk Broads

independent and wild of spirit. Once the police force was established in villages such as these, enforcement became much stronger.

Home of the Roaring Boys

The introduction of schools, often with Church support, and the coming of the railways both also stifled colourful traditions and lawless practices. The enclosure of common land had already put limitations on the activities of highwaymen and smugglers, the latter also restricted by the formation of the coastguard. By the end of the nineteenth century the more out of the way areas of Norfolk were hardly less tame than the rest of the county.

Murder, execution and the Chamber of Horrors

Law and order might have reduced the nefarious activities of certain groups, but there will always be individuals who take the law into their own hands. While poverty and social repression incites justifiable anger, some rebels behave in an extreme way. In 1848 the tenant of Stanfield Hall Farm in Norfolk, James Bloomfield Rush, was evicted because of heavy debt. Even the forgery of documents did not resolve his problem. Finally, driven by insane rage and desperation, he shot both his landlord and his son dead, and wounded the wife and maid. Rush was tried and sentenced to hang at Norwich Castle. The spectacle attracted thousands of people, and Rush also earned a place in Madame Tussaud's Chamber of Horrors.

Sometimes a murder flies in the face of everything for which the perpetrator stands. Just as clergymen have been involved with smugglers or prostitutes, they have also been guilty of crimes of passion. Before his appointment in 1779 as Rector of Wiveton, Norfolk, James Hackman had fallen in love with Martha Ray, an actress and mistress of the Earl of Sandwich. Determined not to err, he followed his vocation but remained obsessed with Martha's refusal to marry him. Driven to distraction, he went to her place of work in Covent Garden and shot her. Following her death, he attempted suicide, but was stopped and subsequently hanged at Tyburn.

The Norfolk bodysnatchers

In the nineteenth century, the resurrectionists, more commonly known as bodysnatchers, murdered for money. Their activities were thwarted by a drive to protect graves from desecration but some, like the notorious William Burke and William Hare, killed solely to obtain the bodies. They were put on trial for profiteering from murder. In 1827 Thomas Vaughan was imprisoned for six months for digging up bodies from a churchyard in Yarmouth, and was later deported to Australia for felony. The strange irony in the

The bodysnatchers

bodysnatchers' story is that these disreputable individuals were in the pay of some of the most respected citizens in the country, the surgeons. Sir Astley Cooper (1768-1841), who was brought up in Great Yarmouth, was one of the surgeons who used the bodies he bought for medical science and to help teach students. Some of those in his pay, who included Thomas Vaughan, were sent to prison. But Sir Astley himself was never convicted. Having received his knighthood for performing a successful operation on George IV, he became Queen Victoria's Surgeon-Sergeant. His position no doubt helped to protect him from official discovery, or at least from prosecution. The story suggests the origin of the theory that Jack the Ripper was a doctor or surgeon connected to the royal family in Queen Victoria's reign. Over the years, many respectable people have had either a dark past or a rebellious streak, as the next chapter explores.

When danger and death haunted the land

As for the 'unrespectable' rebels, they have entered the annals of infamy and, in many cases, romantic or horror fiction. The smugglers of days gone by continue to fascinate people as they did their contemporaries. Unhappy with the restrictions set by 'progress' and the suffering they endured, many people were glad to support the renegades in society. In a world of hardship and poverty, life was cheap and desperation frequently prevailed. Fights often led to fatalities, and murders were commonplace.

Highwaymen were a constant threat to people travelling on land, pirates preyed on those at sea, and death was never far away. Of course theft, murder and smuggling still goes on today in different forms, but crime in Britain is less widespread than it once was, and less conspicuous. As the Norfolk writer L P Hartley said, the distant past is in some ways a foreign land. Norfolk was once as dangerous a place as some of the most deprived places on earth today.

A plaque on the North Norfolk coast

Chapter Nine

KNIGHTS OF NORFOLK UNCOVERED

Knights Of Norfolk Uncovered

THE UNDERBELLY OF THE ELITE

Over the centuries many of those born into high society, or risen to that status, have in some respects cut against the grain of established values. The luckier ones have been ignored or excused, but some were ridiculed or even imprisoned. Even the rich, famous and influential find it hard to ignore the calling of the rebel within, irrespective of the risk of danger or humiliation.

An unconventional poet and priest

In Norfolk during the reign of Henry VIII there were a number of such personalities. One was John Skelton (1460s-1529), a student of Oxford University and Poet Laureate, who coined the phrase 'I smell a rat'! In addition to his appointment as poet to the court of Henry VIII, he was the young king's tutor.

Skelton was a pious and well-connected man, but there was another side to his character. As rector of the south Norfolk town of Diss, flaunting his vow of celibacy and ignoring the approbation of the people, he married and had a child. His parishioners could no longer take him seriously, seeing him as more of an actor than a priest, and after only two years he was compelled to leave.

Despite his court and ecclesiastical connections, Skelton was never slow to voice his disapproval of their greed and wealth. At court, he incensed Cardinal Wolsey, who demanded that he should be imprisoned; Skelton promptly headed for the sanctuary of Westminster Abbey! Earlier, before his move to Diss he had been imprisoned. Though reports do not make it clear, it seems likely his anti-establishment views were the cause.

The doomed Queen

Skelton emerged relatively unscathed in comparison with other high-ranking citizens connected with Henry VIII and court. One of the most famous of these was Anne Boleyn (1501-1536), who was born at Blickling Hall in north Norfolk. Boleyn was related to the East Anglian Howard family that included another of King Henry's wives, Catherine Howard. Like Anne, Howard was executed on the King's orders. Another member of this illustrious family, Thomas Howard, Fourth Duke of Norfolk, was later executed for treason by Elizabeth I (Chapter 4).

Anne Boleyn came to Henry's attention while at court, at the time he was having a relationship with her sister, Mary, and was married to Katherine of Aragon. In order to marry, Henry was forced to defy the Catholic Church, which forbade divorce. After only three years of marriage Anne had failed to produce a male heir and, with his head turned by Jane Seymour, Henry ordered Anne to be executed under trumped-up charges of witchcraft and adulterous incest. It seems likely that Anne's strong, rebellious nature provided the

Blickling Hall, home to Anne Boleyn

encouragement Henry needed to break with his first marriage.

'Nosy Parker'

Her execution imminent, Anne put her daughter Elizabeth into the care of Norwich-born Matthew Parker (1504-1575), who was her chaplain. Despite Parker's closeness to Anne, Henry considered him a law-abiding citizen who did not pose a threat and gave Parker a good position in the church after Anne's death. From childhood, Elizabeth developed respect for Matthew Parker's intellect and moderate views and when she became Queen she appointed him Archbishop of Canterbury.

When visiting his brother in Norwich, Parker is believed to have stood before Robert Kett's 20,000 strong camp on Mousehold Heath in a failed attempt to peacefully quell the rebellion. But in some respects he was less of a conformist or moderate than first appearances might suggest. He was a close associate of Hugh Latimer and Norfolk-born Thomas Bilney (Chapter 4), both of whom were burned at the stake, charged with heresy. A supporter of reform, Parker was himself brought before Lord Chancellor Audley charged with heresy, but subsequently cleared.

Matthew Parker

Like Skelton, Parker broke his vow of celibacy by marrying. His wife, Margaret Harlestone of Mattishall, Norfolk, was the bastion of support Parker needed, and the marriage produced several children. The protestant Queen Elizabeth was among the many that disapproved. But Parker encountered his most severe problems during Mary's reign. As a committed Catholic, she saw his marriage as an immoral affront to the Church. He was forced to give up his position in the church and with his family went into virtual hiding for the duration of Mary's reign.

Parker walked on a knife-edge. Mary was one of many Catholics who hated him for rejection of Catholic doctrine. At the same time, the Puritans also detested him for the religious traditions he upheld. Years after his death, Cromwellian supporters desecrated his tomb. Aware of his many potential enemies, Parker became suspicious, particularly of foreign visitors, to the extent that he would check his silver cutlery after a guest had left to ensure that nothing had been stolen! This habit, together with his investigation of many clergymen through ecclesiastical records, earned him the nickname 'Nosy Parker'– a term still in common usage.

The man who condemned Guy Fawkes

However inquisitive Parker was, for many he would have been preferable to Sir Edward Coke (1552-1634), a prosecutor who took pleasure in imposing harsh penalties. Coke too liked to 'nose out' old information, in his case for legal purposes, and some of Parker's own manuscripts came into his possession.

Born at Mileham in Norfolk, Coke studied in Norwich and then at Cambridge University. A high flyer, he was first a Member of Parliament and then Recorder of London, eventually being appointed to the powerful position of Attorney General. He prosecuted Sir Walter Raleigh and, two years later in 1605, Guy Fawkes and others involved in the Gunpowder Plot. Coke condemned Raleigh as 'the most vile and execrable traitor that ever lived', before ordering him to be taken to the Tower.

Being wealthy, successful and powerful did not stop Coke turning against King James. He was a zealot who believed that Common Law should stand above the King's interests, a view that cost him his seat on the Privy Council. He later regained that position but continued to voice his support for the supremacy of Parliament over the King. Coke was imprisoned for nine months, receiving a taste of what Sir Walter Raleigh had been forced to endure at his behest. Sir Edward Coke's two sons, Sir Robert and Sir Henry,

Thomas Browne

later also suffered imprisonment and sequestration for standing against Parliament. Rebellion was a common thread through Coke's family. His wife stood against him in an attempt to save their daughter from an enforced marriage which was to secure Coke's return to the Privy Council.

Ahead of his time

In contrast to Coke, Sir Thomas Browne's (1605-1682) problems arose from an open, enquiring mind. Browne went to Norwich as a doctor, and lived there for the rest of his life. Widely respected, he received King Charles II as a guest and was subsequently knighted on the recommendation of the Mayor of Norwich.

As an author with a particular interest in science and religion, Browne's challenging theories were frequently the source of consternation. While studying at Oxford and the University of Leiden, Browne would have been exposed to diverse religious ideas. Many dissenting Puritans, including some who sailed to the new colony across the Atlantic on the *Mayflower*, had fled to Leiden for a time. The religious and scientific opinions that Browne expressed in *Religio Medici* aroused anger, especially among Catholics and the book was added to the Papal index of blacklisted writings. Browne was forced to rewrite parts of the book before an authorised edition could be published. Like Thomas Paine, whose views on society and religion had been ahead of his time, Browne's theories of science and religion were too advanced for a society still in the grip of rigid religious beliefs.

From Norfolk to the Dark Continent

Over two hundred years later, another wealthy, knighted Norfolk-based writer also exhibited his rebellious streak. Sir Henry Rider Haggard (1856-1925) was the son of a barrister, born at West Bradenham Hall in Norfolk. He married Mariana Louisa Margitson, also from Norfolk, and after living and working together in the African Transvaal they later settled back in Norfolk. Haggard was respected and a supporter of the British Empire.

The non-conforming side to his nature was perhaps influenced and nurtured by the primal drumbeat of Africa, where many of his books, most famously *King Solomon's Mines*, were set. Just as Haggard's friend Rudyard Kipling had a strong link with India, he developed an intimate connection with Africa and its peoples. His depiction of the ancient Queen Ayesha in the fantasy adventure novel She, which is set in the depths of the 'dark' continent's interior, suggests a fascination with the seductive power of exotic women and it is thought to be based on an affair Haggard may have had with an African woman while in the Transvaal.

The African Queen

Back in England, Haggard expressed his concern about social welfare and agricultural reform in fiction, including *The Poor of the Land*. Like Ada Cole and Anna Sewell (Chapter 3), he was a crusader against cruelty to horses. Though Haggard, like many of his contemporaries, had racial prejudices, he was a man of independent spirit, driven by his convictions to speak out against the injustice he saw.

A man of passion and innovation

Another highly respected Norfolk man, who became romantically involved during his time abroad, was Horatio Nelson (1758-1805). Nelson was born in Burnham Thorpe, and studied at the Paston School in North Walsham. He once said 'I am a Norfolk man and glory in being so'. Dedicated to fighting for his country, he lost an eye in battle in Corsica and an arm in Tenerife and ultimately he died for his country at The Battle of Trafalgar off Cape Trafalgar on the Spanish coast.

Norfolk is proud of its 'Nelson connection', as the 2005 bi-centenary anniversary of the Battle of Trafalgar testified. Horatio Nelson is possibly Norfolk's most famous 'son' and one of Britain's greatest heroes. But he too had an unorthodox side to his character. After his victory in the Battle of the Nile, Nelson stayed in Naples where he met and fell in love with Lady Emma Hamilton. Though both were already married, they soon became lovers. At one point, Horatio lived with Emma and her husband William, who was accepting of the relationship. Conversely, Horatio's wife Fanny was not so accommodating and made it clear that she expected Nelson to give up Emma. The relationship became the subject of jokes and political satire, and was a scandal in the echelons of London society, with the King said to have turned his back on Nelson at one social event. To Nelson's, Emma was his 'wife in the eyes of God'. This was an unconventional view for the times, especially for the son of a rector. Horatio and Emma had a daughter, Horatia, and their relationship continued until his death.

Nelson was non-conformist in other ways too. Legend has him fighting a polar bear; whether that is true or not, we know that he was impetuous enough to become embroiled in the Italian civil war while in Naples and it is believed he was involved in reported atrocities there. Nelson's battle strategies were often unconventional and in defiance of those in authority, but they frequently paid off. By insisting on doing things his way, he won against the Spanish at the Battle of St. Vincent. When given orders with which he did not agree at Copenhagen, he lifted a telescope to his blind eye and reported that the signal was not visible! Following his instincts instead of orders, he won a decisive victory at Copenhagen, which led to his ennoblement. It is reported that he said, 'I may not have the rank but I have moral authority', a reflection of his lack of deference to superiors, as well as his bravery and self-confidence. It was his defiance that created new battle strategies, won the battle on more than one occasion, and helped to make Lord Nelson one of the most important figures of history.

Norfolk's Horatio Nelson

He did it his way!

Sir Douglas Bader (1910-1982) was yet another military figure whose successes in battle were at least in part due to doing things his own way. Bader was based in Norfolk with the Royal Air Force in the Second World War. Having lost both his legs in a plane crash a few years previously, he had managed to resume flying through steely determination. No doubt the same determination lay behind his strong, independent ideas. Douglas Bader took it upon himself to re-organise the 242 Squadron, a move that did not please his superiors. He defended his action before the head of Fighter Command, only to upset them once again in his bid to send RAF fighters out to attack German aircraft in advance of their arrival over British soil. After a new appointment to the head of Fighter Command, Bader's proposal found favour, and resulted in many victories. Ironically, it was while on a mission of this kind that Bader collided with another aircraft over France, and was incarcerated in Colditz for the remaining years of the war. Set free at the end of the war, Douglas Bader went on to high positions in the world of aviation and was knighted in 1976.

A successful rule-breaker

Colin Chapman (1928-1982), who created and developed the Lotus car in Norfolk, attributed his success partly to his compulsion to doing things his own way. As a child, he would defy the rules, taking daring risks on his bicycle and receiving repeated beatings from his school master, a man he and his friends nicknamed 'Fluff Woolly'. As he grew up he would habitually bend the rules or find loopholes to achieve his ends. Cheating and lying apart, he was genuinely innovative and never satisfied with anything short of excellence. His turbine-powered cars were so successful that the United States Auto Club banned them! Chapman went from strength to strength. Lotus cars were sought after by the biggest names in motor racing, including Stirling Moss and Ayrton Senna, and in Formula 1.

Always alert to opportunities, Chapman moved Lotus to Norfolk, where agricultural job losses had created an eager workforce, costs

Colin Chapman's Lotus cars

were lower and the military airfields provided the ideal environment for testing racing cars. The enterprise was based at Ketteringham Hall, which had been the home of Charlotte Atkyns, the 'Norfolk Scarlet Pimpernel' (Chapter 7), and which the US 2nd Air Division had made its headquarters in World War II. Chapman's alleged involvement in the DeLorean scandal in the late

Ketteringham Hall

1970s may have contributed to his premature death in 1982. It was thought that Chapman and DeLorean had personally benefited from part of the millions of pounds allocated by the British government to support the DeLorean car manufacturing business. The truth was never discovered and Chapman suddenly died of a heart attack in the midst of legal proceedings.

Colin Chapman was a very successful man who lived 'at the edge'. From childhood, he was a creative and independent spirit, never keen to follow the straight and narrow.

Independent thinkers

Charles Handy is a controversial and original thinker who does not believe in operating within established rules. A professor of business, and prolific writer and broadcaster, he lives in the Norfolk market town of Diss. Dr Handy is an Oxford graduate who went on to work for Shell International before joining the London Business School and being appointed chairman of School and being appointed chairman of the Royal Society of Arts. Though apparently a 'pillar of society', Handy believes that normal approaches to work and organisational management should be turned on their head, a theory he expounds in *The Age of Unreason*. Within a changing and potentially intimidating world of large corporations, he argues for a new and individual way of working.

Stanley Bagshaw's name lives among the most revered of the editors-in-chief through the history of the *Eastern Daily Press*. A respected Norfolk man, Bagshaw, who was editor-in-chief from 1954 until his untimely death in 1964, dared to challenge the power of Russian communism at the height of the Cold War. He spoke six languages, including Russian. In 1956 when Bulganin and Kruschev visited Norwich, Bagshaw published an article in

Stanley Bagshaw

Russian in the EDP urging the Soviet leaders to allow more freedom of expression and spirit in Russia. Driven by the same sentiments, while on a visit to West Berlin, he made contact with people who were smuggling anti-communist satires across the border into communist East Germany. Stanley Bagshaw championed and supported people in difficulties, especially those suffering political oppression. For instance, after observing the beginning of the Spanish Civil War while on holiday in Spain, he and his wife helped with the care of Spanish refugees in Norfolk. A highly educated and tenacious man, Bagshaw had the knowledge and drive to make a stand for his liberal ideals and, in doing so, earned respect and success.

A man with a calling

Many high profile people are successful as a result of challenging or rejecting what is expected of them. The popular screen and stage actor Sir John Mills (1908- 2005), who was made a Knight of the British Empire in 1977, had to make a firm stand to fulfil his ambitions to become an actor. Born Lewis Ernest Watts Mills, at the Watts Ernest Training College in North Elmham, Norfolk, the young Mills lived for a time at Belton near Gorleston. His father, a mathematics teacher and headmaster, expected his son to follow him into an academic career. At Norwich Grammar School for Boys, Mills preferred sport to his studies and on leaving school he turned his back on an academic life to enrol at a dancing school in London where he trained as a chorus dancer. Spotted by the playwright Noel Coward, Mills moved into theatre and later made his name working with film director David Lean. No slave to convention, Mills became a close friend of the multi-talented Norfolk actor, Stephen Fry (Chapter 6).

The secret ingredient of rebellion

Rebels come in many guises. As these Norfolk examples show, some are prominent figures in society. Their independent spirit and determination have driven them to follow their dreams and achieve success, and sometimes to fly in the face of it. All have had a personal calling that cannot be ignored.

ACKNOWLEDGEMENTS

A big thank you to my sister Amanda, who has worked hard on photos, drawings and the design / layout for this book, and also my mother Ann, her husband John and my husband Steve for all their support and encouragement.

I thank the Eastern Daily Press for the copies of photographs they sent me; Cos Hardy for giving me useful information and a photo; and Anthony Grey and Frank Nolan for talking to me about their thoughts and memories. My thanks as well to Colin, Susan and Simon Chapman for all their help. Special thanks to Jerry Bloom at Wymer Publishing.

ABOUT THE AUTHOR

Joanna Lehmann-Hackett received a BA in Drama and Classics at London University. She has written and directed various film projects. These include *Soulscapes*, an allegorical film about personal discovery and *Change Of Heart*, a short film about a young man who finds a positive alternative to crime. She has written several articles on psychology, mythology, archaeology and history.

Her previous book, *Our Dark Twin* was a venture into the realm of mind and soul. She brings her interest in history and psychology together in Fire In The Veins: Norfolk Rebels.

She now lives in Twickenham with her husband musician Steve Hackett. She has lived in Norfolk and she and Steve regularly visit her family who have lived in North Norfolk for many years.

SELECTED BIBLIOGRAPHY

Atkin, Malcolm: Norwich: History and Guide. UK: Alan Sutton Publishing Ltd, 1993.

bbc.co.uk: The Darkness set the World alight. Feature, 26 January 2004.

bbc.co.uk: Cord pull in worldwide record deal. Feature, 26 August, 2004.

BBC Online: Norwich reflects on National Holocaust Day. 27 September, 2004.

BBC Radio Norfolk: Profile on Keith Skues. 5 October, 2004.

BBC News: Lord Melchett: Aristocrat eco-warrior. 27 July, 1999.

BBC News: Lord Melchett refused bail. 27 July, 1999.

BBC News: You think Norfolk's got problems… 29 November, 2002.

BBC Norfolk: Stephen Fry Interview. 21 March, 2005.

Bewley, Christina and David Bewley: Gentleman Radical: a Life of John Horne Tooke, 1736-1812. *I. B. Tauris, 1998.*

Boyer, Allen D.: Sir Edward Coke and the Elizabethan Age. USA: *Stanford University Press, 2003.*

Boyer, Paul, editor: Salem Village Witchcraft: A Documentary Record of Local Conflict in Colonial New England. USA: Northeastern University Press, 1993.

Brickhill, Paul: Reach for the Sky: Story of Douglas Bader, D.S.O., D.F.C. *Cassell Military, 2000.*

Bruce, John & Thomas T. Perowne, editors: Correspondence of Matthew Parker: Comprising Letters Written by and to Him, from A.D. 1535, to his Death, A.D. 1575. *Parker Society, Wipf & Stock Publishers, 2005.*

Cabell, Craig: Frederick Forsyth: A matter of Protocol. *Robson Books Ltd., 2003.*

Champion, Matthew: Seahenge: A Contemporary Chronicle. Norfolk, UK: *Barnwell's Timescape Publishing, 2000.*

Champion, Matthew and Nicholas Sotherton: Kett's Rebellion 1549. Norfolk: *Barnwells Print Ltd, 1999.*

Church, Robert: Murder in East Anglia. London: *Robert Hale Limited, 1987.*

Clarke, Tony: Pilgrims of the Press: A History of Eastern Counties Newspapers Group 1850 – 2000. UK: *Eastern Counties Newspapers Group Ltd, 2000.*

Collingridge, Vanessa: Boudica. London: *Ebury Press, 2005.*

Corfield, P. J.: Towns, Trade, Religion and Radicalism. Norwich, UK: *Centre of East Anglian Studies, UEA, 1980.*

Cramer, Ketton: Norfolk in the Civil War: A Portrait of a Society in Conflict. London, 1969.

EDP: At home with the Norwich masters. Article by Angi Kennedy, March 18, 2005.

EDP: Norfolk GM crop "to stay". Article by Chris Bishop, July 25, 1999.

EDP: Why Philip Pullman searches for truth. Article by Keiron Pim, March 15, 2005.

EDP: Workers' champion celebrated by lectures. Article by Geoff Pulham, Oct 7, 2002.

Edwards, George: From Crow-Scaring to Westminster. UK: *The Labour Publishing Company Ltd.*

Freeman, Roger A.: The Friendly Invasion. *East Anglian Tourist Board / Terence Dalton Limited, 1992.*

Fry, Stephen: The Ode Less Travelled: Unlocking the Poet Within. *Hutchinson, 2005.*

Grant, Sally: Anna Sewell. UK: *Larks Press, 1996.*

Grant, Sally: Edith Cavell: Nurse and War-Heroine. UK: *Larks Press, 1995.*

Griffiths, Trevor: These are the Times: A Life of Thomas Paine. *Spokesman Books, 2004.*

Guardian, The: Bleak world of the loner who killed. Article by Audrey Gillan, April 20, 2000.

Guardian, The: Time to forgive the Stiffkey 1. Article by John Penny, November 24, 2001.

Higgins, D. S.: Private diaries of Sir H. Rider Haggard. *Stein & Day Publishers, 1980.*

Hipper, Kenneth: Smugglers All: Centuries of Norfolk Smuggling. UK: *Larks Press, 2001.*

Hoare, Adrian and Anne Hoare: The Unlikely Rebel: Robert Kett & the Norfolk Rising, 1549. *Radio Society of Great Britain, 1999.*

Huntsman, Richard: Elizabeth Fry. UK: *Larks Press, 1998.*

Jewson, Charles B.: People of Medieval Norwich. Norwich, UK: *Jarrold & Sons Ltd.*

Johnson, Derek E.: East Anglia at War 1939-45. Norwich, UK: *Jarrold Colour Publications, 1978.*

Knight, Roger: The Pursuit of Victory: The Life and Achievement of Horatio Nelson. *Allen Lane, 2005.*

Lambert, Andrew: Britannia's God of War. UK: *Faber and Faber, 2004.*

Lawrence, Mike: Colin Chapman: The Wayward Genius. UK: *Breedon Books, 2003.*

Leeming, Glenda: Wesker the Playwright. UK: *Methuen Publishing Ltd.*

Lewis, Barry: Kazuo Ishiguro. *Manchester University Press, 2000.*

Logan, Deborah Anna: The Hour and the Woman: Harriet Martineau's Somewhat Remarkable Life. USA: *Northern University Press, 2002.*

Martins, Susanna Wade: History of Norfolk. Chichester, UK: *Pillimore & co. Ltd, 1997.*

Mossiker, Francis: Pocahontas – The Life and Legend. *Da Capo Press, 1996.*

Mottram, R. H.: Buxton the Liberator. London: *Hutchinson & Co. Ltd.*

Murray, Allan G.: American Airmen in Norfolk 1942-1945. Norwich, UK: The Memorial Collection at the 2nd Air Division (USAAF) *Memorial Room, Norwich Central Library.*

Observer, The: The story of his life. Article by Robert McCrum on Ian McEwan. January 23, 2005.

Observer, The: Tuned in, turned out, still far out. Feature with reference to Bruce Lacey. June 6, 2004.

Paine, Thomas: The Age of Reason. London: *Watts & Co, 1938 (first published 1795/1796)*

Pennick, Nigel: Secrets of East Anglian Magic. London: *Robert Hale Limited, 1995.*

Pitman, E. R.: Elizabeth Fry. London: *W. H. Allen, 1889.*

Rawcliffe, Carole and Richard Wilson, editors: Medieval Norwich. London and New York: *Hambledon and London, 2004.*

Rawcliffe, Carole and Richard Wilson, editors: Norwich Since 1550. London and New York: *Hambledon and London, 2004.*

Reynolds, Margaret and Jonathan Noakes: Ian McEwan: The Essential Guide: "Child in Time", "Enduring Love", "Atonement". *Vintage, 2004.*

Richings, Derek and Roger Rudderham: Strange Tales of East Anglia. Seaford, UK: *S. B. Publications, 1998.*

Rushden, Joyce: She Heard Their Cry – The Life of Ada Cole. *Joyce Rushden.*

Sage, Lorna: Bad Blood. London: *Fourth Estate, 2000.*

Snelling, Steve: The Americans in Norfolk during World War Two Over Here. Derby, UK: *The Breedon Books Publishing Company Limited, 1996.*

Storey, Neil R.: A Grim Almanac of Norfolk. UK: *Sutton Publishing Limited, 2003.*

Tate Collection: *Tate Online.*

Tanitch, Robert: John Mills. UK: *Collins & Brown, 1993.*

Timpson, John: Timpson's Norfolk Notebook. Bury St Edmunds, UK: *Acorn Publishing, 2001.*

Tucker, Nicholas: Darkness Visible: Inside the World of Philip Pullman. *Wizard books, 2003.*

Ty, Eleanor: Empowering the Feminine: The Narratives of Mary Robinson, Jane West, and Amelia Opie, 1796-1812. Canada: *University of Toronto Press, 1999.*

Wade-Martins, Peter, editor: An Historical Atlas of Norfolk. UK: *Norfolk Museums Service.*

West, Harold Mills: Little Dick the Smuggler and Other East Anglian Eccentrics. *Barbara Hopkinson Books, 1986, Countryside Books, 2003.*

White, Colin: Nelson. The Pitkin Biographical Guide. Norwich, UK: *Jarrold Publishing, 2003.*

Wise, Thomas J., editor: Bibliography of the Writings in Prose and Verse of George Henry Borrow. *Dawsons Pall Mall, 1966.*

Zelter, Angie: Trident on Trial: The Case for People's Disarmament and the Trident V.3. *Luath Press, 2001.*

INDEX

Lightning Source UK Ltd.
Milton Keynes UK
UKOW01f0651050814

236341UK00001B/10/P

9 781908 724021